BARRON'S PARENTING KEYS

KEYS TO PARENTING YOUR TWO-YEAR-OLD

Meg Zweiback R.N., M.P.H., C.P.N.P.
Associate Clinical Professor
University of California, San Francisco

BARRON'S

Cover photo by Scott Barrow

DEDICATION

To my Mom, for all her support, to Jake and Misha, my two former two-year-olds, and to Zack, for everything.

©Copyright 1993 by Barron's Educational Series, Inc.

All inquiries should be addressed to:
Barron's Educational Series, Inc.
250 Wireless Boulevard
Hauppauge, New York 11788

Library of Congress Catalog Card No. 92-35548

International Standard Book No. 0-8120-1416-2

Library of Congress Cataloging-in-Publication Data

  Zweiback, Meg.
    Keys to parenting your two-year-old / Meg Zweiback.
      p. cm. — (Barron's parenting keys)
    Includes bibliographical references and index.
    ISBN 0-8120-1416-2
    1. Toddlers.   2. Child rearing.   3. Parenting.   I. Title.
  II. Series.
HQ774.5.Z85   1993
649'.1–dc20   92-35548
                                        CIP

PRINTED IN THE UNITED STATES OF AMERICA
456 5500 98765432

CONTENTS

INTRODUCTION: DO "TWOS" HAVE TO BE "TERRIBLE?"

Why is it that two-year-olds are often expected to be terrible? In my eighteen years as a pediatric nurse practitioner I've heard the phrase "the terrible twos" thousands of times, but I've never seen any evidence that this age is any more (or less!) challenging for parents than any other. Nevertheless, when your child achieves this landmark age, you are guaranteed to hear him described as terrible during the year that follows.

Two-year-olds, in fact, are exciting, delightful, and very good company, at least some of the time. The challenges come from their need to explore, to learn, and to become more independent, although they still need their parents to care for them not just physically but intellectually and emotionally as well. As two-year-olds explore the world, they can't judge whether their explorations will endanger their own safety or their parents' peace of mind. When two-year-olds want to learn new things they will often demand that their parents pay constant attention. Two-year-olds have an ever-increasing attention span and memory, and they can get deeply involved in play, often refusing to stop an enjoyable activity when parents want them to stop. As two-year-olds begin to see themselves as important and separate people from their parents, they often assert their independence in ways that seem bossy or provocative. The same characteristics that make a two-year-old delightful will often cause parents to collapse from exhaustion by the end of the day!

In this book, you will learn about the many ways in which your two-year-old will change this year. The first section, "How Your Two-Year-Old Will Grow and Change," describes the way your child develops in the way he relates to his parents, the way he thinks, and the way he learns to use his senses and physical skills to learn. In this section, you also will find Keys about how your child's developmental stage affects his behavior in the daily activities that take up so much of your time together: feeding, sleeping, toilet training, and discipline. Each Key in this section can be read separately, but your ability to understand your two-year-old will be enhanced if you read all of the Keys. Every child is different in the way his development progresses, and each area impacts on another. Developmental steps can occur in leaps or in tiny steps, often with strides forward in one area being accompanied by stalls or slipping backward in another. If you are familiar with the overall pattern you can expect this year, it will be easier for you to understand and anticipate the inevitable ups and downs of your child's development.

The second section, "Temperamental Style," describes in detail the many ways in which children differ behaviorally. All two-year-olds will go through the same sequences of development eventually, but each will do so in his own unique fashion. If you learn to understand your child's style, you may be more comfortable with the ways in which he differs from other children, and perhaps the ways in which he differs from his parents, as well. You also will learn about the child whose temperamental qualities make him more difficult to manage than other children and how you can help him.

In the third section, "Typical Two-Year-Old Behavior and Misbehavior," you will read about the many ways in which you can expect to see your child act in the coming year. You will see how your child's behavior and misbehavior is part of this stage of development, and learn strategies to help you cope with and enjoy the challenges that this not-so-terrible age will bring to your lives.

Part One

~~~~~~

HOW YOUR TWO-YEAR-OLD WILL GROW AND CHANGE

T wo-year-olds are explorers searching for uncharted worlds, scientists investigating the mysteries of nature, poets inventing language for the first time, and psychologists puzzling over the varied ways that people around them behave. A two-year-old is constantly using his intelligence and natural curiosity to expand his knowledge. As parents of a two-year-old you will be amazed at how much your child can learn, and how quickly your child can build on what he already knows. There is no "typical two" when it comes to describing your child's achievements during this year, because the typical two-year-old will be advancing week by week, expanding on his interests and strengths, and learning all the time.

Your two-year-old also is striving to be competent and independent, capable of taking care of himself without any help from you. He will push you away or turn his back to you at times, when you would expect him to want you most, in his desire to declare his independence from you. This inner drive combined with his inexhaustible curiosity form the foundation for your child's future learning. Nevertheless, as the parents of a two-year-old, you may find that at times your child has more energy and motivation than you do! One of the great challenges for parents of two-year-olds

1

is to find ways of balancing their child's needs to expand his horizons with their own needs to create a home and family life that works well for the adults as well as the child. Even as their child is spurning their attempts to help or comfort him, they must wait patiently for the moment he changes his mind.

In this section, you will read about all of the exciting changes you can expect to see in your two-year-old this year, while keeping life safe, interesting, and enjoyable for your whole family.

1

BECOMING INDEPENDENT

ake a few minutes to watch your two-year-old at play. Observe his ability to move his body, to figure out a problem, to manipulate toys, and to talk to himself and to you about what he is doing. Watch the way he feeds himself and asks for more, falls down and picks himself up, and tries to do so much all by himself. Sometimes he asks for help, sometimes he refuses it. He is clearly on his way to becoming a capable and independent child.

Now think back on what he was like just two short years ago—a small, dependent infant who needed you for everything. He depended on you to feed him, comfort him, play with him and to give him all the care that loving parents provide for a baby.

As your baby got older he learned that even though you would be there when he needed care, you sometimes didn't come the moment that he wanted you. He learned that sometimes he had to wait for your attention. He learned that there were other people who sometimes cared for him instead of his parents. He learned that sometimes when he wanted milk he was offered cereal instead, and that if he wanted to play in the middle of the night you expected him to go back to sleep. Sometime in the past year, you realized that he was no longer a baby who commanded all of your attention and concern, and was instead a member of your family. This change may not have been easy for him or for you. As you withdrew the constant attention that you had provided in his infancy, he may have protested. You may have felt uncertain about what he really needed from you, or worried if you felt he needed more than you had to give. Nevertheless, as you moved away from taking care of him at every moment, you saw him learning to do more and more for himself.

A parent learns that it is sometimes difficult to know what a child really needs. A baby needs his parent to feed him for quite a while, but if the parent tries to be in charge of feeding for too long, the baby may start to refuse his meals. A one-year-old will struggle with a parent who tries to change the child's diapers, or put on his shoes, but a parent may have no choice, even though his child acts as though he's being tortured! A two-year-old may cry when his parent leaves for work, but parents realize that he recovers and plays happily with his child caregiver all day.

Last year, your child learned to walk, to communicate his basic needs, and to feel comfortable being himself. At times, you watched him struggle with his desire to be his own person and to cooperate with you. He may have been babyish at times, and very grown-up at other times. You may have felt unable to predict your toddler's mood, whether he would be agreeable or disagreeable. At times, his favorite word may have seemed to be "No!" even when you were sure he wanted to say "Yes!"

Perhaps this description of a one-year-old is familiar to you. Perhaps not. Some children begin to assert their independence from their parents earlier than others. If you have watched your friends cope with some of the stubborn behavior that often accompanies the surge for independence and have been grateful that your own child isn't that negative—be prepared. Asserting independence, often in a negative way, is a part of a child's normal developmental pattern. If you haven't seen this pattern emerge yet, you probably will see it in the year to come.

It's helpful to know that the negativity of a one- or two-year-old is caused by his need to become independent from his parents. However, if your child is in a particularly negative stage of development, it is hard to remember that at this stage, it's positive to act negative! As parents, you can expect to feel frustrated and even exhausted at times, especially when your child seems to be constantly challenging you. If you feel that it is your job to make your child happy at every moment, you may have a particularly hard time this year. A two-year-old needs to know that his parents can be counted on to set limits and to be as reliable and consistent now as they were when he was a baby. If you change the rules every time your child balks, he will probably push you further to get you to take a stand.

As you watch your two-year-old this year, you may feel a mixture of sad and happy feelings. It's delightful to watch him become an independent, curious, lively child. It's also hard to say goodbye to the dependent, parent-centered little one who always needed and wanted your attention. There will be times when your little adventurer wants to stay within the shelter of your lap, but there will be more and more times when he wants to use you as the secure base from which to launch his adventures. Many times he won't know what he wants from you. Many times, you won't know whether to hold on or to let go. You will have to learn by experience, because every child and every family is different. Don't be afraid to make mistakes. The Keys that follow are a guide to help you make better decisions, but your instinct is the guide that will serve you best.

2

HOW A TWO-YEAR-OLD THINKS

Your two-year-old is in love with learning about her world. She has begun to understand that she is a separate person from you and the other people around her, but she still believes that she is the star of the show called "Life." She appropriately sees the world only from her own point of view. Her goal at every moment is to figure out the how and why of everything she encounters and to satisfy her own insatiable curiosity. As her parent, you will be her partner in exploration. She will delight in showing you her discoveries, and through her eyes you may begin to see the world in a new way.

Your two-year-old learns best by direct experience. She is a constant explorer, touching, tasting, smelling, poking, climbing, crawling, reaching up, pulling down, and taking apart. She learns best from real activities and observations, not from explanations or even pictures. She is much more interested in the actions than the results, the process rather than the goal. You may think, "Why can't she finish what she's started?," but she will decide for herself when she has done enough. She may be easy to distract from one interesting activity to another, or she may refuse to budge from a toy that she couldn't be bothered with an hour before. All you can predict for certain is that she will be interested in almost everything at one moment or another!

Parents of two-year-olds find themselves torn between the excitement of watching them blossom intellectually and utter exhaustion at their unending passion for exploration. Because your two-year-old sees the world from her own point of view, not yours, she will not be able to understand it when you don't share her enthusiasm for endless play or conversation.

Your two-year-old may seem interested in listening to you explain the world to her, and may even prompt you to continue your explanations by asking "What?" or "Why?" over and over again. However, even though your child seems to listen to or even repeat your explanations, her understanding of how things work will come mainly from her own direct experience. For example, you might explain to your two-year-old that if she drops her cup of juice it will fall to the floor and make a mess, or that if she drops her cup and makes a mess you will be unhappy about cleaning it up, or that if she drops her cup you will not give her any more juice. She will listen attentively, but she will still experiment to see if everything that you say is really true, from her own experience! In the same way, a two-year-old may listen to explanations of why the sun goes down, or where water goes when you open the drain, or where Big Bird goes when you turn off the television, but she will not truly be able to understand you, because you are describing concepts that she cannot see or touch or experience directly. Your two-year-old's limitations in understanding shouldn't keep you from talking to her about things she is too young to understand. Just try to remember that what is valuable to her is the interaction with you, not the meaning of your explanations.

Most two-year-olds can absorb only a small amount of information at one time. If you give your child a single direction, she will follow it easily, most of the time. If you

7

give her two directions together, she may follow the first one but need to be reminded of the second. If you try to give her three directions at once, it is likely that she won't remember the first by the time you have completed the last one! She may have the same difficulty in making choices: if you offer her a choice between two toys or two treats, she'll be fine. If you add a third choice, she may act confused or upset. That's because a two-year-old, even if she is highly intelligent, cannot always store and remember ordered information the way an older child can.

One concept that your two-year-old will grasp during this year is the idea of "pairs." A two-year-old sees pairs everywhere in her daily life: she has two hands and two feet, two eyes and two ears. She has two shoes and her jacket has two sleeves. Counting to two has real meaning for her. The concept of "two" can be extended to the natural opposites she sees in her daily life: up and down, on and off, light and dark, and, of course, "yes" and "no." You can play many games of matching, counting, and "same and different" that will help your two-year-old to use this concept of pairs and opposites in her future learning. As simple as it may seem, this concept will be fundamental to her learning to read and do math.

What about the two-year-old who has learned to count? Many children can memorize numbers and apply them in a rote fashion, especially if they have learned counting rhymes and games from "Sesame Street" or other television programs. If your two-year-old enjoys counting, by all means count with her. However, if she leaves out numbers or loses track of items, don't correct her or try to help her get it right. The ability to count more than a few objects is beyond the capacity of a two-year-old. If you push her to perform, she may well begin to resist your efforts, especially if her game becomes work instead of play.

One tremendous change that you will observe during this year is her ability to solve problems in her head. For example, a child who at twenty months could pull a simple picture puzzle apart and manipulate or force pieces back together by trial and error will approach the same type of puzzle in different ways at thirty months. Now she is able to remember how the picture looked when the puzzle was whole. She may be interested in watching a parent show her a step in reforming the puzzle. She might listen to a verbal suggestion about trying a piece in a certain spot. She can use different skills and begins to see problems as made up of parts that can be solved one at a time.

As you watch your child at play, you will be able to pick up clues as to how she learns to solve problems. Even at two, many children seem to use certain approaches more than others. Some children are *visual learners*, and will watch and look very carefully before they act. Other children are *auditory learners*, and will ask questions or listen to an explanation offered by an adult or another child. Some children are *tactile learners* and learn best by touching or taking apart. They need to solve a problem by actively working on it. Many children use a combination of all three approaches. By being sensitive to your child's natural learning style, you may be able to help her learn faster and with more enjoyment.

As your child learns to watch, listen, and imitate the actions of people around her, you will see her begin to use these actions in more and more complex play. She will begin to use her own toys or other objects to imitate things she has observed in the world around her. A simple play activity like making a family dinner in a pretend kitchen may evolve into an imaginary party at which her pretend guests not only eat a meal, but act very much like the real people in her life. You may hear your child, as she gets nearer to two-and-a-half, acting out scenes from her daily life, sometimes pretending to be the parent. She may place a real event into an imaginary scene, resulting in a more satisfactory outcome to her.

A two-year-old may also have an imaginary companion, either a special doll or stuffed animal, or a completely imaginary friend who is invisible to everyone but your child. Sometimes these imaginary companions are cooperative sidekicks for your child, but often they are given the role of the "naughty" child, and are allowed to do all of the activities in play that your child knows she is not supposed to do herself. Parents should view this imaginary play as a healthy way for a two-year-old to act out some of the experiences and conflicts of her daily life.

Even though your child can make up pretend stories and activities, she still doesn't understand the difference between "real" and "imaginary." Nowhere is this more evident than in a two-year-old's response to television characters and stories. Since her experience of the world is based on what she can see, that which she views on television is as real to her as that which she experiences in her daily life. In the same way, a two-year-old will respond to the imaginary activities of other children as if they were real-life events. If an older child tells your two-year-old that a monster lives in her closet, you may find yourself dealing with a frightened, sleepless child. A two-year-old also can be upset about real-life figures that adults think of as being friendly—clowns, a Halloween mask on daddy, even a Santa Claus in a shopping mall can be frightening to a child who is sorting out what is and isn't real. If your child seems to be frightened by what you think are "fun" events, you may need to look more closely at these events from a two-year-old's perspective.

From age two to three, your child's ability to remember, to think, and to solve problems will expand at an astonishing rate. Your goal as a parent is to avoid under- or over-estimating what she can and cannot understand. She will change daily and you will have to respond differently to her as she changes. Living with a two-year-old is as much a challenge for you as exploring the real world is for her.

3

THE EXPLOSION OF LANGUAGE

As this year progresses, your child will amaze you daily with his newly found language and speech skills. A twenty-four month old speaks a simple language: many single words and some two word sentences and phrases. He expresses a great deal of interest in labelling people, objects, and actions in the world around him; a two-year-old can drive his parents to exhaustion with never ending queries of "What's that?" But the beginning speech of a two-year-old seems primitive compared to the speech of a child who is almost three, and the rate of change throughout this year is astonishing.

By age two, your child should be expressing himself in speech. Through his responses to your words, he should be letting you know that he understands simple questions and commands. Although his vocabulary may be small, his words should be clear enough that an adult outside the family can understand at least half of what he is saying. This kind of speech is to be expected at the *beginning* of this year. If your child is not talking at all by age two he should have his hearing and speech evaluated by a professional who regularly works with speech and language delayed children. A two-year-old learns by communicating with others and if your child is not able to hear, under-stand, or express himself as well as other children his age, he will not be able to advance in other ways as well. As you read this Key about the speech and language of a two-year-old, keep in mind that although children vary in their rate of developing these skills, the two-year-old who does not speak should be a source of concern.

During this year, your two-year-old will delight you as he expands his vocabulary of words as labels, often with his own pronunciation: "hangurber," "ikesream," and "my byself" are popular two-year-old word scrambles. He will begin using pronouns, such as *me, you, him,* and *her* that he is likely to mix up frequently, especially when referring to himself. He will begin to understand prepositions, such as *on, under,* and *behind,* that he will enjoy learning from you as you play ball or work around the house together: "The ball rolled behind the chair!" or "Let's put lunch on the table!" His ability to use negative expressions also will expand from a simple "no" to sentences constructed with words like *don't, not,* and *never.* He may say, for example, "That not my car."

A two-year-old will use speech to ask complex questions: "Where did sun go?" or "Why she crying?" Sometimes you will be able to answer satisfactorily, and sometimes not. Often, a two-year-old will ask the same question over and over again, causing a parent to think that the answer she gave was not satisfactory. However, a two-year-old may ask you a question repeatedly simply because he *likes* the answer you gave him the first time, and he enjoys having a conversation!

By the end of this year, your not-quite-three-year-old will be able to talk to other adults and have them understand much of his speech, with occasional help from you. As his language becomes more fluent, don't be surprised if he begins stumbling over words at times. He may run up to you in excitement saying, "I saw . . . I saw . . .

I saw . .," pause, and start again. Sometimes he will get more words out and then get stuck. Sometimes he will get so stuck that he forgets what he wanted to say! This stumbling occurs because your child is bursting with ideas, information, and new observations that he can't wait to share with you. His language and vocabulary skills don't flow as rapidly as he needs them to, so he stumbles. If you listen patiently and say, "I know that what you want to tell me must be very exciting," your child will learn to relax and slow down without feeling self-conscious.

During this year, you will see your two-year-old's social skills expand as he notices how other people respond to what he says and how he says it. If you teach your two-year-old to say "Please" and "Thank-you" he will be rewarded by the delighted responses of other adults. That doesn't mean that you should force these expressions on your child—he's still too young to learn good manners unless they are fun for him.

Your two-year-old will learn to recite nursery rhymes and sing songs this year. He will develop a spoken vocabulary of at least 250 words, will use many phrases, and will often speak in sentences. He will use plurals that end in "s" so that he will talk about "books" and also about "mouses." He may also make up his own special words for familiar objects or people in his family, and these special words will often be adopted by the people around him and become part of everyone's vocabulary.

Much of what your two-year-old will learn this year will be learned by listening and observing the adults and children around him. Parents don't need to provide daily speech and language lessons for their young children. However, you can increase your child's ability to under-stand and enjoy communication if you make an effort to encourage your two-year-old's communication interactions. Without thinking about what they are doing, many parents effectively enhance their children's development. The following suggestions help to ensure a good environment for language development:

- Be a good listener. It's sometimes hard for a two-year-old to put all of his thoughts into words. Give him time to say what he wants to tell you. Try not to interrupt him, and don't correct his pronunciation or word order, since his own listening skills will eventually help him to correct himself. Look at your child when he talks, and let him know that you are paying attention.

- Talk to your child about the things that you are doing together, the sights and sounds that surround you, and your plans for the day.

- Help your child to increase his vocabulary and his understanding of language patterns by reading picture books together. Sometimes you can read the words and at other times just talk about the pictures and the story.

- Give your child simple directions and requests to follow as part of routine daily activities, "Go get your shoes," and as part of play, "Let's put the ball on the floor and roll it behind the door!"

- Enrich your child's language by responding to his simple sentences with slightly longer or more complex sentences. If he says, "See the big dog!" you can say, "Yes, that's a big brown dog. Do you want to pet him?"

- Make language fun for your child by making up rhymes and silly words, and by teaching him concepts such as opposites, same, and different through the use of pictures and games.

- Watch children's television or listen to tapes together to get ideas for songs and games that you can use to teach your child about concepts such as counting, colors, and categorizing objects.

The most important activity for parents who want to encourage their child's language development is to display good conversation and listening skills themselves. When you are with your family, try to pay attention to what other people are saying or doing. Keep background noise from music and television to a minimum, because this distraction can interfere with your child's learning to listen and communicate with you. If you are a quiet person by nature, make an effort to talk to your two-year-old anyway, even if it sometimes feels awkward. If you are a non-stop talker or a loud talker, try to quiet down to leave some space for your two-year-old to express himself. This year, as your child learns to talk and to understand speech, much of what he learns will reflect your own patterns of communicating.

4

GETTING STRONG, STAYING SAFE

A s you watch your two-year-old run, can you remember how just a short time ago he hadn't learned to walk? Now, he dashes quickly across the room, down the stairs and even down the street before you have time to say "Stop!" A two-year-old is moving all the time and he is propelled to use his newly coordinated muscles to challenge himself and to challenge you to keep up with him. Of course, he may still have a typical toddler "pot belly" that will make him look more awkward than he really is. As he gets taller, there will be a change in overall posture that will give him the longer, leaner look of a pre-schooler.

Although two-year-olds, like children of any age, will differ in the rate at which they acquire coordination skills, you can expect your child to be walking, running, jumping in place, and jumping over small objects with both feet together by the time he is two-and-a half. If he has the opportunity, he can learn to ride a tricycle or big wheeled trike by the time he turns three. He will be able to balance on one foot for a few seconds and to kick and throw a ball. He will also be skilled at climbing, and this year should learn to climb hand over hand to get up a slide or other ladder-like climbing structure. If you provide him with a narrow board placed flat on the ground, he can learn to "balance" for a toe-heel-toe-heel walk and for simple balancing movements.

Your child can accomplish all of these motor skills barefoot or in rubber soled shoes. He probably doesn't need special shoes even though he may have fat pads on the bottom of his feet that make him look "flat-footed." However, if your two-year-old seems to have an awkward run or standing position because of turned-in knees or bow-leggedness, ask your health care provider to check his legs to reassure yourself that his posture is typical for his age.

Safety should be a primary concern for parents of two-year-olds who are testing the limits of their strength and skill. A two-year-old can't anticipate danger, but is old enough to follow rules that you enforce. Your rules should include what your child is and is not permitted to do.

For example, since you can assume that your two-year-old will often need to run, try to provide him both with safe places to unleash his energy and definite rules to follow when the surroundings are not safe. Most parents find that there are places in their neighborhoods with enough open space to be able to let their child run and play and "blow off steam." He'll enjoy himself more if you play a game of "tag" or "chase" or take a large ball with you to have a simple game. You may be lucky enough to be near a park with a climbing structure or other equipment designed for small children. When you take your child to any public play area, whether it is designed for young children or not, be sure to inspect the area for any trash, sharp objects, or other debris that could be dangerous. An area that has sand should be fenced or covered to keep animals out, because two-year-olds are likely to put sand and sand toys in their mouths and animals can contaminate sand with their wastes. Play structures, swings, or slides should be placed over a soft surface such as grass, sand, or deep redwood bark to provide a cushion should your child fall. If you have questions about the safety of the play areas in your community, begin by calling your local health department: you may then be referred to the agency that handles these questions.

Two-year-olds will often dart away from you as you walk down the street or when you are in a parking lot or in an open space such as a shopping mall. Running away from you can put them in danger of being hurt or being lost. Parents find different ways to control highly mobile toddlers in these situations:

- Before going to an area where you expect your child to stay quietly at your side, stop somewhere to let him run. If you are going to be walking on a busy street, park two blocks away so that he can run first. If you are going into a store or mall, give him time to run around at home or at a park before you get there.
- Have your child sit in a stroller when you know that he will have trouble staying next to you or is likely to run off to investigate his own interests.
- Teach your two-year-old to hold onto your hand on busy streets and in parking lots. Since your hands will sometimes be full, teach him to hold on to your pants or skirt fabric as a substitute. If you want your child to follow this rule, be sure to remind him of it before you begin your walk or get out of the car.
- A two-year-old who is not willing to stay in a stroller and who will not hold your hand can be allowed some freedom of movement without being in danger if you attach a cord from his wrist to yours. You can buy or make velcro wrist-bands with telephone-type spiral cords between them for parent and child. Although some parents feel that these cords are like "leashing" a child, a parent who has had a near-miss accident with an active toddler may welcome the added security. Don't

use the cord as a punishment—just give your child a choice between holding on to your hand or the cord.
- If you find that your two-year-old is always running off and you are always having to scold or restrain him, it may be better for both of you to avoid situations that are "set-ups" for misbehavior. If you can find a place for him to stay while you go shopping or on errands, you'll both be happier.

Two-year-olds can become very skilled at climbing, so they need opportunities to climb safely. Indoor and outdoor structures work best for daily exercise. Should you have the space in your home for an indoor structure you will find that your child makes excellent use of it and that it will make bad weather less of a problem for both of you. However, your child may still climb up on counters, bookcases, or furniture that you want to be off-limits. You should put latches on doors that lead to balconies, steep stairs, or areas of your home that are dangerous. If you try to store cleaning supplies or medicines in a high cupboard without latching the door carefully, your child may decide to climb up to see what was so interesting that you had to store it out of his reach! Dangling electrical cords or tablecloths are particularly dangerous for toddlers, because they are tall enough to reach and pull, but not tall enough to see what might come crashing down on their heads. When you have an active two-year-old, you cannot make your home completely child-proof, because his skills and curiosity will exceed your ability to anticipate what he will do. You will have to supervise him all of the time.

A particular danger to active, curious two-year-olds is water, whether in a bathtub, a garden pond, or a swimming pool. Most parents don't realize that a young child can drown in as little as two inches of water. There are more drownings and near-drownings among two-year-olds than any other age group. Even a child who has been taught rules about water safety will often lose his balance at the side of a pool or decide to "practice swimming" in the tub if he is left alone in the bathroom. An open toilet or a bucket of water is a danger to a curious toddler. Parents sometimes think that teaching a toddler to swim can protect him, but a toddler's coordination is not enough to keep him afloat, especially if he is frightened. It's a good idea to be aware of potential water hazards in your home and neighborhood, and in places where you go to visit or on vacation. Although fences, covers, and alarms will reduce the danger of water, there is still no substitute for close adult supervision when a two-year-old is involved.

As parents watch their two-year-olds becoming stronger and more coordinated day by day, they often wonder about taking them to sports or exercise classes to develop their motor skills faster. Some of these classes can be great fun for parents and children together. However, there is no evidence that a two-year-old will benefit from early instruction or exposure to sports or gymnastics. If you decide to take a class, observe the instructor ahead of time to be sure that the expectations of toddler behavior are appropriate (children should not be expected to stand in line for a turn or to sit quietly for more than a few minutes). If your child wants to keep going to class, he's probably getting something out of it, even if he's not getting a head start on an athletic career!

5

BUILDING HAND-EYE
COORDINATION

Your two-year-old's improved hand-eye coordination, combined with her increased memory, makes it possible for her to experiment and explore the world around her in new ways. For example, a one-year-old might play with a simple shape sorter over and over again in the exact same way, enjoying the repetition of the task. A two-year-old, however, who has gradually learned how to fit different shapes into matching holes, will often remember the steps she has already learned and build on her previous experiences. Parents are often amazed at how quickly two-year-olds can master increasingly complex motor tasks. This mastery comes from their new ability to retain information that they have experienced directly.

However, it is important for parents to remember, as described in the Key "How a Two-Year-Old Thinks" that a two-year-old cannot usually generalize her experience from one area to another. Her mastery of one type of toy will not necessarily make it easier for her to use a similar toy without practice. That's why it is still necessary for a child this age to have many opportunities to play with the same materials repeatedly, and why a two-year-old will enjoy playing with toys that seem to the parent to be almost identical. For a two-year-old, even the smallest variation in an activity makes the activity "new" to her.

If you watch the way your two-year-old uses her hands, you will see some significant differences between what she can do and what a younger child can do. She can use her fingers carefully and precisely, and has more control over the use of her whole hand. A two-year-old can feed herself with a small spoon or fork and most of the food will wind up in her mouth. She can probably open a container with a lid or unscrew the top of a jar, and many two-year-olds can open the "child-proof" medicine containers that frustrate adults! She can hold a crayon and scribble in large and small circles, and can judge the size of a piece of paper if you ask her to keep her coloring within the edges (it is still best to have her color on a washable surface, however!). A two-year-old can often watch an adult's hand movements and imitate the action she sees very precisely.

Your child is likely to show a preference for one hand, but she may also change back and forth from left to right. There is no reason to encourage the use of one hand over the other, and there may be a disadvantage to your child's overall development if you pressure her to use a hand that she does not prefer.

Hand coordination skills are a result of increased fine-motor skills, but they are also a result of the child's increased ability to look at what her hands are doing, to think about what she is doing, and to think about the results of her actions. This ability is called hand-eye coordination. This coordination will improve gradually. Your child's level of coordination will be determined by both her neurological development and by the opportunities she has to play with and practice on a variety of different objects that you can provide for her.

Your two-year-old will enjoy playing with toys that fit together and can be pulled apart: small blocks, plastic toys that lock together, simple puzzles with four to six pieces, or toys that can be stacked or strung together. A two-year-old will enjoy the process of manipulating these toys, and will enjoy your participation in the play. However, she may play with the toys longer and learn more from them if an adult does not show her how to "make something" or how to "do it the right way." Since many toys for toddlers come in packages that show how to make objects out of the materials provided—for example, how to link plastic bricks together to build a truck—a child or her parents can feel frustrated if it is too hard for the child to build the specific object. It's often a good idea to put the illustrated toy boxes away and to let your child keep the toy in a plain container that doesn't restrict her idea of how to use the toy. A young child doesn't need to "make something" to feel successful in her play.

Two-year-olds will be very different in their preferences, so it makes sense to let your child play with toys at friends' homes before buying out the toy store. It's often possible to buy toys at garage sales or in toy consignment shops, where parents bring their older children's out-grown toys to recycle. Here are some toys that most parents find their two-year-olds love:

> Interlocking plastic blocks
> Large beads to string on thick strings with rigid tips
> Shape sorters with round, square, and triangular holes and blocks
> Wooden blocks in all sizes
> Fat crayons
> Wooden or plastic trains and trucks
> Puzzles with pieces that fit into marked shapes
> Housekeeping toys: dishes, utensils, pots and pans, pretend kitchen
> Office toys: telephone, computer, calculator

Tool toys: plastic hammers, nails, screws, and wrenches

Dolls and stuffed animals

Of course, there are hundreds of toys that a two-year-old will enjoy, and most children will accept as many toys as you give them. However, many parents find that if a child has a room or toy box loaded with toys, she is likely to ignore most of them. If you have many toys, think about bringing a few different ones out every week and putting away the ones your child seems to play with less often. Stored toys can be rotated and will seem like new when they reappear in a few months. Instead of using a toy box with a lid (which can be dangerous if the lid falls on a toddler's hand or head), keep the toys out on shelves so that your two-year-old can see them and be reminded of her choices.

Your two-year-old will build her fine motor coordination and perception skills in many ways other than playing with toys. You can show her how to point to objects in books, to trace the outlines of shapes with her finger, and to practice skills like pouring water into glasses and filling containers with sand. Your two-year-old will learn from every experience, and you can help her learn by giving her encouragement every time she tries something new. Of course, you will also have to put up with her being slow or messy as she tries to master these skills, but in the long run, a patient parent makes it possible for a child to become more competent.

6

~~~~~~

FEEDING

Whether or not your two-year-old has a good appetite, it is likely that you will have some concerns this year about what he eats, when he eats, and how he eats. The feeding relationship between parents and children is sometimes complicated when parents worry about whether they are offering their child a nutritious diet. In addition, even when parents feel confident about their food choices, their child may not be willing to eat the way parents want him to!

The typical two-year-old will sit with his parents at the table, in a high chair or a booster seat, and be able to manage much of his feeding on his own. Of course, that doesn't mean that he will feed himself with a great deal of skill. He will probably prefer to use his hands rather than a spoon or fork, and if he is given a large portion of any food he may decide to play with it rather than eat it. If parents are uncomfortable with the messiness of feeding time, they may prefer to try to feed their child themselves or to correct his table manners as he eats. These approaches can cause a child to become a reluctant or resistant eater, so it's better to gradually teach your two-year-old by modelling good manners yourselves and by using child-friendly equipment to make the job easier.

Offer your child very small portions of foods that are easy to pick up in his fingers or sticky enough to cling to a spoon or fork. Put the food on a non-breakable plate with edges or dividers that he can push the food against to get it on the utensil. Experiment with small size tableware with handles that fit his grasp. A two-year-old should be able to hold a small cup or glass, and can usually manage to drink without spilling if you don't put in more than an inch of fluid. When your child attempts to feed himself, praise him for being a big boy, but don't scold him when he makes a mess. Try to treat spills casually, saying "Uh-oh" and allow your child to help you mop up afterwards. If you get upset about every accident, you may find that mealtimes become unpleasant. In fact, if you make too much of a fuss about your two-year-old's mealtime behavior, he may start to spill or throw his food just to get your attention.

If your child seems to throw or spill his food when he's finished eating, watch him carefully so that you can catch him at his first gesture. Say "All done?" and if he says, "Yes," take his food away. If he has already thrown his food, use the same words without making them a question. Take his food away, say "All done," and take him down from his chair. If he protests, you can try again, but if you find that he continues to throw or spill the food purposely, it's better to end the meal.

Some two-year-olds throw food repeatedly during a meal, not because they've finished eating, but as a way to get a parent's attention. A young child doesn't think of mealtime as a time for pleasant conversation about the day. He'll enjoy sitting with you as long as he's entertained, but should he get bored you can expect him to misbehave in order to get you to react. There are a number of ways to avoid this misbehavior. Some parents plan an early meal with their young child, so that they can teach him to sit quietly while the parent talks or reads to him. The adult mealtime and conversation takes place at another time. Other parents manage to eat with their child by keeping their own conversation to a minimum and trying to include the child as much as possible. Of course, there are some children who enjoy sitting and eating quietly while their parents talk, but at this age this behavior is usually a result of the child's personality rather than parental training.

Even if your child's mealtime behavior is pleasant, you may be worried about whether he is eating well. When you were growing up, your parents did not have as much information about nutrition available to them as you do now. They also didn't have as many foods from which to choose as they planned the family meals. As you decide what to feed your own child, you may find that your beliefs about good nutrition are different from those of your parents, or that your ideas about healthy foods are different from those you hear from experts or from food manufacturers' advertising. It's important to remember that even though many of our ideas about good nutrition have changed over time, some basic principles and common sense will help you sort out what is right for your two-year-old.

All children need to eat foods that provide enough energy for both their daily activity and their need to grow. The foods must also supply them with the nutrients that we all need to keep our bodies healthy: protein, carbohydrates, fats, and vitamins and minerals. It's not necessary for parents to calculate the recommended grams or milligrams of these nutrients into daily menus. It's much easier to offer your child a variety of nutritious foods, allowing his tastes to guide you. Most two-year-olds will eat three meals a day and at least two to three snacks as well. Even if your child doesn't eat very much one day, he will probably eat more on another day.

In order to plan for feeding your two-year-old, you'll need to know the types and amounts of foods he needs for good nutrition. These guidelines will help you to plan the meals and snacks he needs daily.

Dairy Products   3 servings a day, equal to 1 cup of milk or yogurt, 1 ounce of cheese, or ½ cup of cottage cheese. If your two-year-old doesn't have a big appetite, limit milk to 2 cups a day.

Grains   At least 5 servings a day of bread, rice, pasta, cereal, tortillas, or other grains. A serving is about ½ ounce in dry weight, so a cup of dry cereal and a ½ cup of cooked rice are equal in nutrition.

Fruits   2 servings a day of a medium size piece of fresh fruit or 4 ounces of juice, plus one 4 ounce serving of a Vitamin C rich fruit or juice. If your two-year-old drinks more than 8 ounces of juice a day he may not have an appetite for other nutritious foods.

Vegetables   3 servings a day of 2 tablespoons. Offer a dark green or yellow vegetable as one choice.

Protein   2 ounces a day, for example, 1 ounce meat and 1 ounce fish, or 1 tablespoon peanut butter and 1 ounce chicken. If a child does not eat any animal protein, his diet should be reviewed by your health care provider. Include an iron source, such as meat, legumes or iron fortified cereal.

A child who is offered foods from these groups will get a well-balanced diet that is rich in the nutrients he needs to grow. If he is offered one or two small portions of sweets or fatty treats a day, these will not interfere with his appetite for the nutritious foods. However, if he regularly snacks on foods that are high in sugar or fat, he will be less likely to want to eat other foods. Sugar and fat are ingredients that make foods taste good, and a two-year-old who gets used to chips and cookies may learn to prefer them to the taste of whole grains and fruits.

Many two-year-olds will go on "food jags" for weeks or even months at a time, refusing all vegetables, or only eating spaghetti without sauce. Parents can urge, cajole, beg, or even force their child to eat other foods, but a two-year-old under this kind of pressure will usually become more resistant. If your child seems to be so narrow in her food choices that she eliminates one of the food groups for more than a few weeks, you can give her a vitamin and mineral supplement to make up for the missing nutrients.

Parents who are concerned with their children's long term health may consider encouraging healthier eating habits that limit the fats and cholesterol in foods that can contribute to heart disease in adult life. The meal plan described here is consistent with the recommendations of the American Academy of Pediatrics and the American Heart Association. Both groups feel that in order to limit cholesterol intake, children should not eat more than three to four eggs per week, and that extra fat in a child's diet should be limited. However, two-year-olds should not be on restrictive diets and should be allowed to eat all of the recommended foods in whatever quantity they request.

7

‿‿

SLEEP

Some two-year-olds fall asleep easily at the end of every day and sleep throughout the night. Some two-year-olds take naps regularly and without resistance. If your two-year-old is a "good sleeper" you are lucky, because the majority of two-year-olds are frequently awake when their parents would like them to be asleep! A large number of two-year-olds will frequently have trouble falling asleep or staying asleep without having a parent nearby.

A two-year-old who is happy during the day will often be very unhappy when you tell him the day is over. He is too young to understand the concept of time, so when he says good night he cannot really comprehend that a new day will begin again soon. He is also too young to understand that if he stays up late at night he will have trouble waking the next morning. He is definitely too young to understand that he gets wound up or cranky when he is overtired. In fact, for many two-year-olds there is truly no good reason to go to sleep at night, unless they drop from exhaustion or their parents make it very clear that it is bedtime. Unlike an infant who will usually nap throughout the day to get a sufficient amount of sleep, a two-year-old may resist sleep even when he is tired and wind up chronically overtired. A chronically overtired child may seem to be irritable or grouchy, and he also may be more susceptible to illness.

Two-year-olds need to sleep about thirteen hours out of each twenty-four hour period. This is an average amount, based on the patterns of many children. Your own child may need more sleep or less sleep than this average. A good way to find out how much sleep your child requires is to keep a record for several days of how many hours he sleeps when you allow him to wake up on his own. Add the number of hours of nighttime sleep and daytime naps, and divide by the number of days you have recorded. This figure will be your own child's average daily need. You sometimes can tell if your child is getting enough sleep at night by his ability to wake himself in the morning. A child who is getting enough sleep will not need his parent's help to wake up and will usually be cheerful even if he is slightly groggy.

Most two-year-olds will have some of their sleep needs met by a nap during the day, usually in the early afternoon, that lasts one to three hours. Some children can be helped to sleep longer at night by having naptime limited during the day. Children who take a very late nap will sometimes stay up later at night and sleep later in the morning. Depending on the parents' schedule, this delayed sleep cycle can be an advantage or a disadvantage.

Most parents would like their two-year olds to go to sleep early enough in the evening for the adults to have some private time together. To make your child more cooperative at bedtime, you can help him to learn a routine and pattern about falling asleep that makes it easier for him to let go of the pleasures of his day with a minimum of fuss. In addition, it will help if he has seen you enough during the day to be willing to say good-bye at night. When parents and children are very busy all day and only begin to interact at bedtime, it is often hard for all of them to let go of each other's company. So the first step in helping your child to sleep well at night is to be sure to make time for family fun earlier in the day or evening.

Two-year-olds who have a regular bedtime routine are far more likely to fall asleep easily than children who have an unpredictable evening pattern. For most young children, the bedtime routine will take about a half hour. Some parents spend several hours in activities with their children before bed but don't label any of the activities as "bedtime." However, it is usually easier for a child to settle down to sleep if there is a short series of activities that signal, "After this, I am expected to go to sleep." These activities should be relaxing rather than stimulating— wrestling and pillow-fights tend to excite children and make it hard for them to fall asleep. Bedtime routines often include a bath or washing face and hands, changing into pajamas, telling or reading a story, singing a song, and saying good night to parents with hugs and kisses. Many children and parents develop special sayings ("I love you. I love you, too. I love you, three.") or rituals such as saying good night to all the stuffed animals or pictures in the room. Often, a child will want to sleep with a special blanket or other object. Night lights or dimmed overhead lights help a child to bridge the transition from day to night. Some children enjoy listening to music. These routines can provide a child with the security and relaxing repetition that can help him to fall asleep. By limiting the time spent on these routines, most parents can stay calm and relaxed themselves. This is important, since most parents find that, should they act rushed or tense at bedtime, their child responds by resisting rather than cooperating.

Most two-year-olds can fall asleep in a crib or bed without a parent staying with them. If parents do stay, they should watch for signs that their presence truly is helping the child rather than keeping him awake. Some two-year-olds become aware that once they fall asleep the parent leaves. In order to keep the parent from "disappearing," they fight sleep and rouse themselves each time they start to drift off. Other children may fall asleep easily at bedtime when the parent stays with them but wake during the night and call the parent to help them fall asleep again. If your child has developed one of these patterns, read the Key "Difficulties at Bedtime and During the Night."

It is common for two-year-olds to express fears at bedtime. The relaxed time with a parent gives the child an opportunity to talk about real or imagined worries and experiences he has had. When your child talks to you in this way at bedtime, you should listen and be warmly affectionate and responsive, because these fears will usually be lessened if a parent is comforting. By listening to your child and reassuring him calmly that you will keep him safe, you will help him to relax and go to sleep. If he seems to be elaborating on his fears as you listen, you can tell him that you will talk more in the morning, but that he must go to sleep now. If these fears and bedtime worries appear occasionally, respond to them as they come up and take them in stride. However, if your child seems to have persistent fear or anxiety at bedtime, even if he seems fine during the day, it's a good idea to discuss the pattern with your health care provider. Persistent fears may be an indication that something else is troubling your child.

Parents are often unsure about when to take a child out of his crib. A two-year-old can stay in a crib until he begins to climb or jump out of it. At that point, it is unsafe to keep him in it and he should graduate to a bed or a mattress on the floor. To keep him from rolling onto the floor, use a guard rail or, if the bed is alongside a wall, place a tightly folded blanket between the mattress and box-spring or frame so that the bed tilts slightly towards the wall.

34

The biggest disadvantage of taking a two-year-old out of his crib is that he is likely to get up and wander during the night. It's a good idea to have a gate at the door to his room or at the top of the stairs and at bathroom entrances to protect him. Some two-year-olds will wander into their parents' room at night. Often, parents find the toddler in bed with them in the morning and don't remember his arrival. If you don't want your toddler to join you in bed, you can prevent him from coming in by putting a gate at his bedroom door or your bedroom door. Some parents compromise by having a sleeping mat next to their bed for their toddler. This type of nighttime awakening is very common and should not be seen as a problem unless the parents' sleep or privacy is disturbed.

Even though many two-year-olds resist naptime, most of them still need to sleep during the day. It can be hard for busy parents to provide the kind of middle-of-the-day structure that helps children to nap, but this time can be a welcome break for both parent and child. Most parents find that unless they have a routine, it's hard to get an active two-year-old to nap. Some parents can vary the time, and some children will fall asleep in a car or stroller, but the majority of two-year-olds do best with a set time and place for naps. Naptime routines do not need to take as long as bedtime routines, but they should follow the same pattern of soothing activities followed by some rituals. Many parents find that playing a tape of music or stories helps the child to lie down quietly and gradually drift to sleep. As a child gets older, he may stay awake to listen to several tapes, but he will still have the pattern of an afternoon rest time.

If you talk to other parents about their two-year-olds' sleeping patterns, you will hear many variations. Parents of more than one child find out that their children's sleep habits vary as much as all of their other characteristics. You may find that your child's patterns vary throughout the year, sometimes in response to daily events, and sometimes because your child is growing and changing. The way you manage your child's sleep now is unlikely to make a difference to him or to you six months or a year from now. However, if you and your child are sleeping better at night, you will probably enjoy your days together more.

8

~~~~~~

TOILET TRAINING

I f your child has turned two, he is probably ready to begin using a potty chair or a toilet and to start being in control of his patterns of passing urine and bowel movements. Just as children are different in other ways, so they differ in the way they become trained to use the toilet. There is no approach to toilet training that will work for every child, but there are guidelines that you can follow to help your child to be trained successfully in the shortest time with the least difficulty on your part.

Begin toilet training by observing your child for signs that he is developmentally ready to control himself. Parents used to believe that a child who was trained early was either smart or had competent parents. We know now that toileting behavior is not related to intelligence, and that putting pressure on a young child to use the toilet before he's ready often causes a child to rebel and resist the training for a longer period than if the parents waited. Pediatrician T. Berry Brazelton, who studied more than a thousand young children, found that when parents waited for signs of child readiness, most children were daytime trained by twenty-eight months of age, and virtually all were trained by three years.

A child who is ready to be toilet trained will be aware that he has wet or soiled his diaper and also may be aware of the feeling he has when he is in the middle of urinating or having a bowel movement. An observant parent can watch a child's face and body expressions when he seems to be filling his diaper and comment on what she sees, "It looks like you're making a poop right now." Once a child can recognize these body sensations, his next step will be to learn to recognize when he is *about* to pass urine or have a bowel movement. Some children will be able to label and announce these feelings early in their training, but others will need their parents' help to notice that they "need to go."

As your child is learning these feelings, it is helpful to avoid making negative comments about his messy diapers. A two-year-old feels that what he has produced in his diaper is a part of him. If you frown and complain about having to change him, he may assume that you disapprove of him too. Instead, praise him for telling you when he needs to be changed and compliment him if he helps you by handing you a diaper or being cooperative. You can talk approvingly about big children who use the toilet and wear underpants, but don't criticize toddlers who don't, or your child will worry about your judging him the same way.

In addition to making positive comments about other children who use the potty or toilet, you can also read to your two-year-old some of the many books available about making the transition from diapers. When you choose a book, be sure to find one that is written at the same level of language and complexity as those your child already enjoys.

It's a good idea to get a potty chair for your child to get used to, even if you aren't quite ready to begin training. He can begin by sitting on it with his clothes on at first, and you can tell him that someday he'll be able to use it as the big kids do. You will have to choose between a small seat that rests on the floor or a seat that can be placed directly on the toilet. When you make your selection, consider whether you need a potty chair that can be moved about the house or to other locations, and whether the style you like is easy to clean. It's important that your child be comfortable in the seat and that he be able to rest his feet on a hard surface while he is "going," so you may want to let him come with you to check for size and fit.

Next, start dressing your child in clothing that he can manage to pull down on his own, ideally pants with elastic waists and skirts for girls. Overalls and jumpsuits look cute, but a two-year-old can't manage them independently. Even though your child will still need a lot of assistance from you at the beginning of training, you will want to encourage him to feel capable and in control. If he needs you to help him with his clothing, it reinforces his feelings of being small and baby-like.

Wait for a time to begin training when your life can be fairly routine and stable for several weeks, if not longer. That doesn't mean that you can't have any stresses or unusual circumstances, but because training involves learning new patterns, it's best if he doesn't have to learn in a variety of settings, at irregular hours, or with many different people present. Some families have successfully trained children when they are on vacation—the setting may be new, but the family is relaxed and moving at a slower pace than usual. Though you may not be able to wait for a perfect time, don't plan to begin training if the family is experiencing a disruption such as illness, difficulty between parents, or severe emotional distress.

Begin potty training by removing your child's diaper and having him sit on the potty for two minutes several times a day. If you choose times that you've noticed he usually passes urine or a bowel movement you're likely to help him feel successful. Good times to try are when your child has just awakened, after a meal or snack, and before bath time. It's a good idea to keep the potty chair in the bathroom most of the time to reinforce the idea that using the potty is like using the toilet, just like big people do. Stay with your child, just talking or perhaps reading a very short story. Make the times brief and don't force your child to sit if he doesn't want to. It's helpful if both parents supervise toileting, so that it doesn't become one parent's job.

After a few days, weeks, or months, depending on your child's style, you will find that he is frequently producing something for the potty chair and seems to be wetting or soiling his diaper less often. This is the time to stop using diapers and to start using cloth underpants while your child is awake. Some parents feel safer using the padded training pants to prevent the outside clothes from getting wet, but the chance to wear colorful decorated underwear is a powerful motivation for some children, so you may want to have some of each.

Once your child is out of diapers, have him go to the potty chair at regular, frequent intervals. Most children will need to "try" every $1\frac{1}{2}$–2 hours in order to stay dry. It is often helpful to set a timer, so that the buzzer or bell "tells" the child to go, rather than the parent. Praise your child for every effort, and comment favorably if he produces, but don't get too excited. You want your child to feel that using the potty or toilet is evidence of how competent he is. If you go overboard with praise and congratulations, he will start using the toilet just to please you—or worse, refuse to use the toilet to show you that he's the boss of his body.

Some children do like the motivation of charts, stickers, or even small prizes for using the potty. A reward for toilet training usually works best because the child was completely ready and willing to be trained anyway, and the reward was the boost he needed to take the leap ahead. You can use these methods, but if they don't result in rapid training, you should probably discontinue them.

Once your child is wearing underpants part of the time, it's helpful to move all bathroom related activities into the bathroom. Have him remove and change his diaper or pants in the bathroom, dispose of them in a basket or hamper, and clean himself, with your help, in the bathroom. Some children will want to flush the toilet, but some will want parents to flush for them. Try to stop using a changing table to dress him, and move his clothing into drawers or baskets that he can reach without your help. By creating an overall atmosphere that supports your child's desire to be competent in caring for himself, you'll promote his desire to be big. That doesn't mean you can't help him at all, but help him in the way you would help him to do any other task around the house, by being supportive and encouraging, and not critical.

If you have a boy, he may want to urinate standing up. If he does, provide him with a stool to place in front of the toilet. Teach him to lift the seat and put it down after he is done. You may want to put a sticker in the toilet bowl to help him learn to aim.

For most children, toilet training goes smoothly if the pace is left up to the child. However, some children begin to resist sitting and will argue or refuse the parent's request to go to the bathroom. If you feel as though your child is beginning to battle you about using the toilet, it's best to stop training for a while. Tell your child that you can see that he doesn't want to be trained yet, and that you're going to take a break. Don't blame or belittle him. Tell him that every child learns to use the potty, and that he will too, someday. Put him back in diapers, and try again in six to eight weeks.

41

If either parent begins to be upset about a child not being trained, it can be helpful to make an appointment with your health care provider to discuss the issue. Talking with someone who has seen many two-year-olds and their parents can be very reassuring. In addition, you may be able to get some help in developing an individualized plan for your child. Some children also respond very well to a discussion with an outside person about the advantages of being toilet trained.

Once your child is out of diapers for his waking hours, you should expect that he will have occasional accidents. Accidents are likely to occur when he is absorbed in a game or activity and doesn't "go" when he feels the urge, or when you are in a new place and he isn't sure where the bathroom is. You can anticipate these situations by reminding your child to go to the bathroom, and by visiting the bathrooms of stores, restaurants, and other people's homes when you first arrive. Even with all of these precautions, most children will have accidents for three to six months after the time when they seem to be trained. If your child begins to have regular, frequent accidents, however, consult your health care provider to rule out a medical reason, such as a urinary tract infection.

9

~~~~~~

DISCIPLINE

Parents of two-year-olds react to the word discipline in different ways. For some parents, this word means punishment. Other parents feel that it means to be very strict. Even though the word has negative connotations for many people, the word discipline actually means teaching and training. Most parents would agree that it is their job to teach and train their child to behave in a way that makes life enjoyable for the child, the parents, and for other people in the child's life. If that is your goal for your child, then you will want to teach him in a way that is appropriate for his age and in a way that gradually will help him to learn to control his own behavior. In this Key, you will read about an overall approach to discipline that may work very well for you and your child. Later in this book, you will find examples of typical behavior and misbehavior of children in this age group, and you will see how the techniques described here can work in your daily life.

An approach to discipline and behavior management needs to be balanced in the same way that diet needs to be balanced. No one technique will work all of the time. This approach works because it encourages good behavior but assumes that there will be times when you will have to interrupt your child's misbehavior. This approach to discipline includes three areas, as the following diagram shows: realistic expectations, modifying the environment, and setting limits.

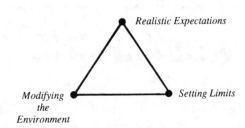

Realistic Expectations

If your expectations for your child are realistic, his behavior will be less frustrating for you. Two-year-olds can be expected to behave in certain ways that are typical for their age. As you read this book, you will see that much of your child's behavior and misbehavior is a result of his drive for independence, his curiosity, his activity level, and his limited ability to think through the consequences of his actions. However, if you begin teaching him now, by encouraging his good behavior and discouraging his misbehavior, he won't be acting like a two-year-old when he's five!

The most important thing to remember about your two-year-old is that he cannot tell the difference between good behavior and misbehavior unless you teach him. Most two-year-olds naturally behave nicely much of the time. However, unless you make a point of praising your child when he is behaving the way you want him to, he may not learn to enjoy the feeling he gets from knowing that he has pleased you. Children who are praised and acknowledged for what they do right are more motivated to behave well than children who are only scolded. Even if it feels awkward to you, get in the habit of saying to your child, "Good for you!" or "I like the way you did that!" as often as possible. *Catch them being good* is a useful phrase to remember if you sometimes feel that you are always criticizing your child's behavior.

It's realistic to expect that your child will have difficulty cooperating or following rules when he is in a new situation, or when there are other disruptions in his life, such as visiting relatives, a new baby, or a change in baby-sitters. Many children seem to have difficulty during transition times such as arriving home from childcare or leaving the playground.

Parents need to have realistic expectations of themselves as well as their child. When parents are over-scheduled, under stress, or having trouble organizing their own lives, it is likely that they will have trouble dealing with their children. Parents sometimes say that they struggle more with their two-year-olds on days when they are very busy than on days when life is more relaxed. Parents also say that it is easier for them to manage their children's behavior when the adults in the family have a similar approach to discipline. Although parents do not need to agree about everything, when their views on child-rearing conflict, their child may misbehave just to watch mom and dad disagree! Parents who were raised in families where discipline was either very harsh or overly permissive may try to avoid repeating the mistakes they feel their own parents made. Should you want to raise your children differently than you were raised, you cannot just decide what *not* to do. You will need to spend time finding a new approach that feels comfortable and works for you and your child.

Modifying the Environment
A two-year-old will behave best when he is in an environment that is safe and appropriate for a child his age. An active child needs space to run and climb, indoors and

out, or he'll be jumping on the furniture and climbing on the counters. A curious child needs you to remove dangerous temptations and breakable objects so that he doesn't have to hear "no" all the time. A lively and intelligent child will have an easier time behaving if he is provided with toys and activities instead of being expected to sit quietly without constant attention. A child who has a daily routine is usually more cooperative than a child for whom life is very unpredictable.

In addition, most two-year-olds behave better when they are cared for by adults who take an occasional break. A parent who is always "on-call" for a child can become tired and irritable, especially at the end of the day. If a parent shares the care of a child with other adults—relatives, friends, or babysitters—the child usually benefits because the parent is more rested and relaxed.

Setting Limits

Setting limits effectively is one of the hardest tasks parents face. Most parents find that it generally is not difficult to set limits in order to protect their child's safety. For example, most parents are able to make a two-year-old sit in a car seat, although the child may resist at times. Most parents are able to prevent a child from turning the dials and knobs on the stove, even though a child may want to help in the kitchen. However, most parents say that it is more difficult for them to set limits in areas that are less clear-cut than in the area of safety. For example, it can be very hard to keep a two-year-old strapped in a stroller or grocery cart, or to restrict him from playing with the dials and knobs on the television or stereo equipment. Though the situations are similar, it is easier for parents to be firm and consistent when the consequence of breaking a rule is that their child would be in danger. Not surprisingly, a two-year-old learns which rules he must always follow, and which ones he can challenge!

The first step in being effective at setting limits is to decide what rules are important to you. A good way to decide what rules you want to emphasize is to make a list of all positive and negative behaviors you would like to encourage or discourage in your child. Both parents should make separate lists. You might include behavior that is dangerous (such as running into the street), destructive (such as throwing toys), hurtful (such as hitting), or particularly annoying (such as throwing food on the floor). Look over what you have written, and choose a few behaviors that you think are the most important for now. These will be the behaviors to begin setting limits on. After you have become successful in setting limits on these behaviors, you can choose others from the list. By making changes slowly, you and your child will be more successful in the long run.

Next, make a clear rule about each behavior that you can communicate to your child: "You must hold my hand when we walk down the street." "You may not throw toys." "No hitting people or animals." "No throwing food on the floor." Make sure that your child hears the rules by looking him in the eye, touching his shoulder, and speaking slowly.

Once you have told your child the rules, it is your job to make sure that he follows them. A two-year-old can't control his own behavior very well, but you can provide him with a limit-setting structure that will help him to build self-control over time.

First, frequently remind your child about the rules you have made, especially when you see that he is about to have an opportunity to follow or break the rule: "When we get out of the car, I want you to hold my hand while we walk down the street." "Here are your blocks—remember to put them down gently. No throwing." It is helpful to tell a two-year-old briefly the reason for the rule. "It's safer if you hold my hand." "When you throw the block it can hurt someone or break something." However, most two-year-olds will not follow a rule because of the reasoning behind it. A two-year-old doesn't think that way yet, but if you explain the rules to him over the next few years, he will learn!

When your child follows rules you've made, always take notice. It's easy for parents to take good behavior for granted and to only respond to misbehavior. A child can learn quickly that he gets more attention for acting naughty than for acting nice! Let your child know that you are paying attention to the positives: "You did a good job of sitting in the grocery cart." "Good for you for remembering to hold my hand." "I like the way you waited for your turn on the slide and kept your hands to yourself." Some parents feel uncomfortable about complimenting a child, but parents who use this technique report that the more genuine compliments they give, the more good behavior they see in their children.

If you see your child about to misbehave or to break a rule, try to interrupt his actions by redirecting or distracting him. For example, a child who has his arm raised to throw a toy can be told, "If you want to throw, here's a soft ball." If you can see that your child is about to dump his carrots on the floor, scoop up the carrots and give him a piece of bread instead. If you see your two-year-old about to grab a toy from another toddler, offer him a different toy and give him your full attention for a moment. When your child looks as though he's about to misbehave, tell him a funny story, sing a song, move to another location, or do what you can to help him to forget his original plan and move on to behavior that is acceptable.

If you aren't able to redirect or distract your child (and there will be many times when you can't), you will then have to stop him from misbehaving. One method is to provide direct consequences for your child's misbehavior. Sometimes you can stop him most effectively by removing whatever object or activity is causing the problem. For example, if your two-year-old throws a block, you take the block away, saying, "Remember, no throwing blocks." You can then give him another toy. If he throws that toy, take it away and issue the same reminder. Sometimes this simple response will be enough. At other times, your two-year-old may be in a more provocative mood. Instead of removing the toys one by one, you may need to remove him from the setting and get him involved in another activity. If you stay calm, your child will not feel that he is getting extra attention for misbehavior and may be able to stop throwing. Other direct consequences might be putting a child in a stroller if he won't hold your hand, taking him away from the table if he throws food on the floor, or taking him out of the sandbox if he hits another child. In each case, your child learns that the consequence of misbehavior is that the activity he was enjoying will be interrupted. Over time, he will learn to stop himself before he misbehaves.

Although you may use all these techniques, your two-year-old will still challenge you on occasion. There will be times when you feel that his misbehavior requires a stronger response. In the next two Keys, you will read about Responding to Misbehavior and also about how to use time-out techniques for the times when setting limits gently does not seem effective.

10

~~~~~~

RESPONDING TO MISBEHAVIOR

I t's a fact of life—your two-year-old will misbehave. Although you may be able to manage much misbehavior by using the techniques described in the Key on discipline, your two-year-old will need a stronger response from you at times. That's because two-year-olds are at a stage in life when they are declaring their independence from you, and part of their declaration is to challenge your authority as the rule-maker. At times, a normal two-year-old will break rules that you have explained clearly. At times, a normal two-year-old will break rules while looking at you with a smile as if to say, "Who, me, misbehave?" At times, a normal two-year-old will break rules and look at you defiantly as if to say, "So do you think you can stop me?" This rebelliousness is to be expected—it's a natural part of this stage of development. Your success in managing this behavior depends on your response.

In my work with families, I have heard from thousands of parents about how annoyed, irritated, and angry they feel when their children misbehave. These feelings are common among parents of young children, and it's easy to understand why. It's hard work to deal with the demands of a child's daily needs without the extra work of having to stop a child from repeatedly misbehaving. Often, parents react to their child by yelling, warning, slapping, or spanking him in an effort to stop the misbehavior. But when I ask parents, "Do these methods work?" most of them sigh and say, "Sometimes, but not usually." In fact, parents often tell me that even when the methods work for the moment to stop the misbehavior, both the child and the parent feel bad afterwards.

There are different methods of responding to misbehavior, each with its own advantages and drawbacks.

• *Yelling*
It would be hard to find a parent who never yells. If your child is used to hearing you speak to him at a certain level and you raise your voice in pitch and volume, he's likely to pay more attention to you. If you sometimes give your child a command or reprimand in a forceful, stern voice you will probably find that this tone is highly effective in helping your child to understand that you mean business. However, if you are also acting excited or looking very angry when you raise your voice, you may find that this approach is less effective, especially if you are yelling frequently. That's because a two-year-old is sometimes trying to see what will happen if he provokes you, and when you lose control of your voice he feels as though he is in charge of *your* behavior rather than the other way around. After a while, you may find that you are yelling more and he is paying less attention to you. If you are going to yell, try to raise your voice firmly and authoritatively rather than screaming with anger. Some parents find that if they take a few deep breaths or count to ten before saying anything they can control their voices better.

• *Warnings*
Some two-year-olds will stop their misbehavior when a parent reminds them in a firm voice what will happen if they don't stop: "If you throw the block again I will take

it away." "If you don't hold my hand you will have to leave the store." However, many two-year-olds don't pay any attention to threats or warnings because they have learned that the parent doesn't do anything after giving the warning. If you are in the habit of warning your child when he misbehaves, watch yourself the next time you respond this way. You may find that your words are just stalling tactics that postpone your having to take another action. You may even find that the more warnings you give, the more your child misbehaves. It's as if he was saying, "Stop talking and do something to show me you're in charge!" If you find that your child usually changes his behavior after the first warning, then this technique may work for you. But if you find that one warning is rarely enough, it's time to try something else.

* *Slapping and Spanking*
Does it work to hit a child when he misbehaves? Some parents think it does. Certainly, a child who is in pain is very likely to stop whatever he was doing while he cries. Some children will stop misbehaving in response to a gentle slap on the hand or on the bottom. Other children will ignore a slap but can be stopped by a harder spanking. Parents who use these techniques often use them because their own parents slapped and spanked them and they feel that the approach is useful. In this country, many parents approve of slapping and spanking children to control their misbehavior. However, there are problems with hitting children that parents should consider.

When a parent spanks a child, the child learns a very powerful lesson. He learns that his parent is bigger and stronger than he is and can hurt him if he disobeys. For this reason, many children will stop misbehaving after parents slap or spank them. However, the child who is hit may also be learning other lessons that the parents didn't intend to teach: "It's OK to hit if you don't like what someone else is doing." "It's OK to hit instead of using words when you are angry." "It's OK to hit someone who is smaller than you are." When a child learns these lessons at home, he is likely to take what he has learned from his parents into the world. Children who are hit at home are likely to hit others at school or on the playground. They are also more likely to hit their brothers and sisters. When they grow up, they are more likely to hit their own children. Sometimes when parents tell me that their own parents hit them I will ask, "When did they stop hitting you?" The answer is often, "When I started hitting back."

If you do use slapping or spanking as a way of controlling your child's behavior, it's important that you protect your child from physical injury. If you hit, keep your hand open and *never* use a fist. *Never* hit a child on the face or head, and never shake him, since that can cause a serious whiplash injury. *Never* use an object to hit: switches, belts, brushes, and wooden spoons can inflict much more damage than you might expect. If you leave a mark on your child's skin, you are hitting too hard (and in most states you will have crossed the line between corporal punishment and child abuse). If you find that you are hitting your child often or hard, or you are feeling out of control when you get angry, call the number in the resource section of this book. For an alternative to hurting your child, read the Key that describes the time-out technique.

11

TIME-OUT

As you learned from previous Keys, a two-year-old is very likely to challenge her parents with repeated misbehavior. All the understanding, preparation, and child psychology in the world will not prevent you from having to interrupt her misbehavior forcefully and firmly at times. In this Key, you will learn about the time-out technique, a simple but effective way for a parent to stop a child's misbehavior. The time-out technique is not a substitute for planning ahead to help your child to follow rules, or for providing a safe and child-friendly environment, or for being sensitive to your child's need for approval and attention at all the times when he is behaving well. The time-out is an additional technique to use when other techniques are not effective.

A time-out is used when a child breaks an important family rule that is either hurtful to the people around him (such as hitting), dangerous (such as climbing on a high counter top or pulling the cat's tail), or deliberately provocative (such as spitting or throwing sand). A time-out should be used when you know that your child has learned the rule but is still breaking it.

A time-out is not just a punishment. A time-out gives a parent a way to use more than words to interrupt a child's misbehavior without hurting the child. A time-out is an effective tool that can be used in almost any setting. The key to its effectiveness is that the parent takes action *without* getting excited, emotional, or angry. As you read in the Key on responding to misbehavior, if your two-year-old learns that her misbehavior can cause you to act upset, she may continue to provoke you, just to test her own power over your emotions. If you stay calm, she will see you as being in charge and in control.

How a Time-out Works

When a child breaks a rule, the parent calmly reminds her of the rule: "No hitting" or "No pulling the cat's tail." The parent then says, "You have to have a time-out now." Then, without further discussion, the parent takes the child to the time-out spot. The spot can be a chair in a corner, a stair, the end of a sofa, or the child's room. If parents are away from home, they can substitute a park bench, the back seat of the car, or a chair in another part of the room or house where they are visiting. The child must stay in the spot for a *very* short time—two minutes is plenty for most two-year-olds. The parent should stay with the child to keep her there, and may need to hold her. At the end of the time-out the child may resume play. If the child breaks a rule again, the parent should repeat the time-out. A determined child may continue to misbehave in an attempt to push a parent into losing his temper. If the parent stays calm and is consistent, the child will eventually become bored by the repetitive interruptions.

Difficulties with the Time-out Method

Some children will sit quietly throughout the time-out, but others will cry or protest. Some children will kick and scream or have a tantrum. No matter how your child responds to the time-out, it is important for you to stay calm. Even if she is still crying or protesting at the end of the two minutes, end the time-out. Keep in mind that your job is to teach your child that her original behavior was unacceptable. If you enlarge the area of conflict to include her reaction to the time-out by punishing her for crying or having a tantrum, she will forget the reason you started the time-out in the first place!

If your child runs away from the time-out place, calmly walk her back. You may have to do this several times. You may need to hold her. Even though this method is simple, it can be very hard work. It is a measure of a child's strength, drive for self-control, and persistence that she can struggle against your calm authority at this time. If your child's anger at you is strong, you may get angry yourself. Keep in mind that you want your child to learn to imitate your calmness, not to feel that she can get you to imitate her tantrum.

Some parents feel overwhelmed by the intensity of a two-year-old's response to this method. They feel that it is sometimes out of proportion to the misbehavior that caused the parent to use the time-out in the first place. They may even feel that other methods, such as spanking or shouting, take less time than the time-out method. However, parents who use this method report that even a child who initially struggles vigorously will eventually calm down and stop repeating the original misbehavior. Even more important, the child whose parents use time-outs as a method of punishment do not see their parents needing to become loud, angry, or violent to assert their authority.

After the Time-out

When the time-out is over, give your child a brief hug and move on to another activity. You may want to distract your child from the original misbehavior by taking her to another room or offering her a different toy. Some children will recover quickly from a time-out, but others will look sad or act defiant. If you are just beginning to enforce a rule that you have let slide in the past, your child probably will test you again in a few seconds or minutes. You may have to begin all over again! The time-out method works because most children eventually realize that it is not very interesting to sit with a boring, calm parent every time they misbehave. You may need to call on a great deal of patience and endurance, but if you can outlast your child, you'll eventually win her cooperation—until she thinks of a new way to challenge you!

Part Two

~~~~~~

TEMPERAMENTAL STYLE

T wo-year-old children are alike in many ways, but like all people, they differ from one another in many ways. As you watch your two-year-old with other children his age, you may see behavior that makes you wonder, "Why does he act like this?" He may laugh louder or race about more than the other children. He may want to stay by your side long after the other two-year-olds have gotten busy with toys and activities. He may be unpredictable in his need for rest when all of your friend's children still seem to need a regular afternoon nap. Sometimes the differences we observe among children are a result of different styles of parenting. Often, the differences are due to inborn qualities of a child, qualities that have been present since birth.

From the time a baby is born, certain behavioral patterns can be observed that will continue to be part of that child's behavioral style throughout his life. These patterns are influenced, but not completely changed, by the responses of parents and other family members, caregivers, and friends.

Your child's inborn behavioral style will have a big effect on how he learns and interacts with his environment and with you. His style, which is also called his *temperamental style* or *temperament* may determine how easy or difficult he is to care for at different stages of his life. If you recognize some of your own temperamental qualities in your child, it may be easier for you to understand his behavior. However, if your child's temperamental style is one that clashes with yours, you may find it perplexing and difficult to understand why he acts the way he does. Whatever your child's temperamental style, understanding it will help you to understand your child and get along with him much better.

In this section, you will learn about nine different temperamental qualities. Qualities of temperament were first described and studied by two researchers at New York University, Stella Chess, M.D., and Alexander Thomas, M.D., both professors of psychiatry. Chess and Thomas observed differences of behavior and development among a large group of healthy, normal babies, and continued to observe these babies as they grew into children and adults. Their observations spanned thirty years, and they were able to show that a child's inborn temperamental differences were critical factors in determining the child's overall behavior. Their work has been expanded upon by many researchers and clinicians who work with young children and their families. Some excellent books on temperament have been written for parents, and are listed in this book's Suggested Reading and Resources section.

As you read about each of these qualities, you will see how recognizing your child's unique characteristics can make it easier for you to understand and help him as he grows.

12

ACTIVITY LEVEL

Almost all two-year-olds seem active to adults. Now that your toddler has mastered the skills of walking, running, and climbing, she often finds it hard to sit still. Some two-year-olds, however, are more active than is typical for this age, and some two-year-olds are very inactive compared to others.

Most parents begin to notice their baby's activity level by the time she is a few months old. A very active baby is often squirming around in her cradle before she is old enough to roll over. By the end of the first year, she can't be left alone because she can crawl or toddle into trouble in an instant. The baby with the lower activity level behaves very differently. She is usually content to sit on a blanket or in a stroller for long periods and seems to be happy just watching the world move around her or playing with toys within her reach.

Just as some babies are *very* active or *very* quiet, so are some two-year-olds. It's valuable to think about your child's natural level of activity because this quality will affect the way you can expect her to behave in many situations. The active child needs to be able to move as much as she needs to see and hear. Even though all two-year-olds seem to climb and run and move around for short periods, the more active child will need to spend more time in energetic play. The quieter child will play and then take a break and be able to sit quietly for longer periods.

Here are questions to ask yourself about your child to get a sense of how active she is:

Does my child always struggle to get moving while I dress or diaper her?

Does my child run when she moves through the house?

Does my child squirm and move around while she is waiting for food?

Does my child have trouble sitting for long periods of time in a shopping cart in the supermarket?

Does my child fidget when we're having a quiet activity, even though she's interested?

When my child is playing with toys indoors, does she move about and throw and bang her playthings?

Does my child enjoy activities that involve moving around more than activities that require sitting?

If your answers to most of these questions are a strong "yes," you have an active child. If you answered "no" most of the time, your child is more quiet. Most parents will have answers that fall in between two extremes but will see their child as generally either active or quiet.

If your two-year-old is active, your daily life together will be more manageable if you provide her with frequent opportunities to move around. An active two-year-old can't sit still for long periods, no matter how firm you are or how much you scold her. It's helpful to have an area of your home set up for her to run and jump and climb. If you provide your child with a safe play structure and pillows and mattresses for her to jump on, you won't have to spend as much time telling her not to climb over the furniture. If you want to take an active child to a restaurant or on a shopping trip, be sure to give her time to exercise her muscles before you go somewhere where she must be quiet.

If she can't sit still, it's best to remove her from a situation rather than to try to force her to behave the way you'd like. Try to remember that an active child's movement is not misbehavior. She may be able to understand that you want her to be still, but a two-year-old doesn't have enough self control to contain herself for long. By keeping your expectations low and the amount of time for which she must be quiet short, you can gradually teach her to be able to sit still longer.

Many active children have at least one parent who is also very active. If your own temperamental style is on the quiet side, you may find your toddler's activity level particularly demanding. If you can remember that the high energy movement of your child can be a real asset as she gets older and needs less supervision, you may find it easier to appreciate her now.

A child who has a low activity level is usually seen as being well behaved or very mature because her quiet behavior is easier to manage. A parent who is very active, however, may be frustrated by a child who prefers to sit in the sandbox rather than run around at the park. A two-year-old who is inactive will often prefer to be pushed in a stroller or carried, and it can be hard for a parent to decide when to insist that the child walk. Just as the parent of an active child can't make her sit still, you won't be able to force your quiet child to move. If you encourage short walks and try to find physical activities that your child enjoys, you will be more successful than if you are always pressuring her to catch up or to play with other children. Take advantage of the positive aspects of this temperamental quality by sitting quietly together reading books and playing games, or by taking her on strolls through stores or museums that other parents of more active children have to avoid!

13

REGULARITY

A child who is predictable in his daily patterns and physical habits has the temperamental quality of regularity. A highly regular child can be expected to fall asleep at the same time every evening and wake up at the same time every morning. He is usually hungry at a regular time each day, and his parents can predict the amount he will eat at certain times. He often has his bowel movements at a predictable time of the day, also.

Since so much of a two-year-old's life is planned around these daily routines, a regular child can be cared for easily by his parents. The only disadvantage to this regularity occurs when parents would like their child to change his schedule. For example, if a highly regular two-year-old is invited to a birthday party that starts right at his nap time, he may not be able to postpone his nap to go to the party. In contrast, an irregular child will be much less predictable in his daily patterns. He may not act sleepy even though he has been awake and active for hours and his parents think he needs a nap. If he does fall asleep, he may nap for a half an hour one day and several hours another. His appetite is unpredictable, and he may eat very little one day and act as if he is starving the next. His pattern of bowel movements is equally unpredictable and he may skip days or have several movements in one day.

Here are some questions to ask to determine your two-year-old's regularity:

- Does my child seem sleepy at about the same time each evening?
- Does my child wake up at about the same time each morning?
- Does my child want to eat about the same amount of food at each meal every day?
- Does my child have a routine snack during the day or at bedtime?
- Does my child seem to be very active or very quiet at predictable times each day?

If your answers to most of these questions are a strong "yes," then you have a highly regular child. If you answered "no" most of the time, your child is more irregular. Some parents notice that their child is more regular in some ways than in others.

If your two-year-old is very regular, you probably have been able to arrange your life around his schedule. If his schedule matches yours, your lives have been more ordered because you can predict from day to day what he will need. He may be less likely to resist taking naps or going to sleep at night. Frequently, he is easier to toilet train because his parents know when to expect him to need to "go potty."

At the same time, you may sometimes have felt locked in by your child's schedule. You may have noticed that your child is unhappy if you disrupt his routine, and you may find that parents of less regular children don't always understand why you can't be as spontaneous or flexible as they are. Fortunately, as the regular child gets older, even though he still may be predictable, he will become more able to adjust his schedule for special occasions.

If your child is very irregular, it's possible that you also have characterized him as a terrible sleeper or a fussy eater. You may have noticed that your child's unpredictability is part of a pattern. If your child seems to be irregular now, and you can remember that he was irregular even as a baby, you may need to modify your family life to impose some order. If you establish a schedule for an irregular child and enforce it gently on a daily basis, he will gradually become more predictable. Your lives may become more enjoyable together, even if his irregular quality is not changed, only tamed. For example, parents of an irregular child can decide on a regular time and routine for going to bed, even if their child sometimes stays awake playing in his bed. They can arrange regular meal or snack times, so that their child learns that food arrives on a schedule, even if he chooses not to eat. An irregular child may be more difficult to toilet train, especially in regard to bowel movements, so parents should be careful to wait until their child is showing definite signs of readiness before beginning training.

Although the irregular child is very challenging for most parents in the early years, his lack of an inner clock can be an advantage to him as he gets older and more independent. His irregularity may make him able to be more flexible and accepting of the natural unpredictability of the real world!

14

~~~~~~

RESPONSE TO NEW SITUATIONS

Young children vary greatly in their response to a new situation. Some children act as if they are instantly comfortable when they meet new people or are taken to a new place. Other children seem to pull away or withdraw when first meeting someone or entering a new environment. Many children initially will hold themselves back, perhaps staying close to their parent. Then they gradually open up and seem comfortable.

When a two-year-old has a pattern of seeming comfortable with new places and people, she is displaying the temperamental quality of approachability to new situations. The child who seems to welcome newness is often seen as well-adjusted, since this open quality is one that is valued in American society. Though this quality may be inborn, her parents will probably feel proud of their outgoing child and pleased with themselves for encouraging her sociablity. On the other hand, the child who withdraws or turns away from newness is often labelled as shy. Parents are sometimes told that they are responsible for this behavior, perhaps because they have sheltered their child or because they are overprotective. Even though parents may know that their child needs them to help her manage newness, they may wonder whether letting her act naturally is helpful to her.

Here are questions to answer to determine if your child's initial response to a new situation is generally one of approach or withdrawal:

- Does my child smile right away when an unfamiliar adult talks to her?
- When visitors come to our home, does my child approach them?
- Will my child talk right away to an unfamiliar adult?
- Does my child want to explore new places right away?
- Does my child want to play right away with children she meets away from our home?
- Does my child seem comfortable within ten minutes in most new situations?

If your answers to most of these questions are a strong "yes," then you have a child who has an eager response to a new situation. In general, you will find it easy to take her to new places and feel comfortable that she will enjoy herself. Do keep in mind that a friendly, outgoing two-year-old can wander away from you in a store or shopping mall. Sometimes outgoing children need very careful supervision to keep them safe.

If your answers to these questions were mostly "never," then your child may take her time becoming comfortable with a new experience. If your child is given adequate preparation and support for new experiences, she can learn to adjust as happily and successfully as any other child. However, if you criticize her or push her, she is likely to become clingy, withdrawn, and perhaps even fearful.

If your child tends to withdraw from newness, take the time to figure out what kind of experiences seem to be the most difficult for her so that you can help your child to cope with them. Although some two-year-olds enjoy going to new places, your child will probably prefer to visit places she has been before. The more often she visits a friend's house, the sooner she is likely to get off your lap and play. She will probably find it easier to play with one or two other children rather than in a big group, although she may like to go places where many children are playing if she simply is allowed to watch. Try to talk to your child ahead of time about new places or people that she will be seeing and let her know that you will stay with her as long as she needs you. With time and repeated experience, she will develop more and more self confidence.

Don't feel embarrassed or defensive about your child's response. Should someone say to you, "Why is she so shy?" don't accept their label. Instead, let your child hear you respond, "She's not shy. She just takes her time. She's very observant, watchful, and discriminating. That's her style."

15

ADAPTABILITY

C hildren react differently to new situations both in their initial response and in the time they need to adjust to change *after* their first response. The temperamental quality that describes this time of adjustment is called adaptability. A child who quickly feels comfortable with new routines or in a new setting is adaptable. A child who takes time to accept change or new routines is less adaptable. The less adaptable child requires a great deal of patience from his parents to help him accept change.

Parents of an adaptable child usually find that once he has tried something new a few times, he acts as though he's been doing it his whole life. For example, even if an adaptable child is initially hesitant to visit a play group, by his second visit he seems comfortable and at ease. The less adaptable child, on the other hand, will take much longer to get comfortable, and his parents may have to bring him on repeated visits before he will feel at home.

At home, the less adaptable child takes time to get used to new rules and routines. Parents can feel frustrated when a less adaptable child continues to act as though he hasn't heard a rule he has been told several times, or resists a new routine for days. The less adaptable a child is, the more he will resist or protest when any change is introduced into his life. He's not trying to be difficult, it's just that change is hard for him.

Here are some questions to ask to determine if your child is adaptable or less adaptable:

- Does my child take several days to get used to being in a new place?
- Does my child seem uncomfortable with other adults even after he has been with them several times?
- Does my child take a long time to get used to being left with a new baby-sitter?
- Does my child have trouble sleeping in a new place for the first several times?
- Does my child resist a change in daily routines, even if I explain the change to him ahead of time?
- Does my child continue to misbehave in the same way even though I have set a clear limit several times?

If your child is fairly adaptable, you will have answered most of these questions "no." If you have answered "yes" to some or all of them, your child is probably much less adaptable than average.

An adaptable child is often easier for parents to manage because he adjusts so quickly to change. However, parents of a very adaptable child sometimes forget that even though their child can cope well with change, he may still be happier if he has predictable routines in his life. For example, even though it is easy to go visiting or travelling with an adaptable child, he still may become overstimulated by new experiences. He may wind up being cranky or even having a tantrum if you push his adaptability beyond his limit.

Parents of a less adaptable two-year-old will have to balance their child's need for predictability and routine in his daily life with his need to learn to adapt to change. You cannot always avoid new experiences, and even if you could, your two-year-old needs some new experiences for variety and stimulation.

Parents of a less adaptable child have to get used to offering their child new experiences repeatedly in order to overcome their child's resistance to change. For example, you may find that you have to offer your child a new food many times before he is willing to taste it. You may have to take your child to the same park for weeks before he'll be willing to play with the other children. If you leave your child with the same baby-sitter over and over again, perhaps several times a week, he will get used to being cared for by someone else. Whatever it is that is new in your child's world, if he is less adaptable he will need time to adjust. By giving him repeated opportunities and lots of gentle encouragement, he will learn that change is a part of life that he can adapt to successfully.

16

INTENSITY OF REACTION

An intense child expresses her feelings with passion and gusto. When she is happy she shrieks with laughter, and when she is distressed she erupts in tears or outbursts of screaming. A child at the other end of the spectrum of intensity can be described as mild. A mild child expresses herself with soft or subdued reactions. If she is happy, she smiles or simply looks content. If she is unhappy, she frowns or gets tearful, but she is generally quiet in her protests.

If your child is intense, you know that you have a child who is hard to ignore. You probably take great delight in the enthusiasm and joy she expresses when she is happy. Her passion for enjoyment will often make her the center of attention with adults and a natural leader of other children. At the same time, however, you may find that her way of expressing anger or sadness is hard to take. An intense child can get so involved in her own feelings that you cannot comfort or talk to her until her storm of feelings has subsided. If you are an intense person yourself, you may find that her outbursts trigger an equally intense response from you. You may find it difficult to stay calm when she is losing control, If you are a mild person yourself, you may feel overwhelmed and uncertain when your child is bursting with emotion. You may wonder if you should do something to calm her or placate her, even though she doesn't seem to respond to your efforts.

A child who is mild is often easy to get along with. When she is angry or rebellious, she may express herself in ways that are quiet compared to other two-year-olds. You may have to urge her to let you know whether she likes or dislikes something, because her reactions are not obvious. If you are a mild person, you may find it easy to understand your child's low key reactions. On the other hand, if you are a more intense person, you may need to pay special attention to the more subtle ways in which your child expresses herself.

Here are some questions to ask to get a sense of whether your child is generally intense or mild in her reactions:

- Does my child laugh loud and hard when she is tickled?
- Does my child kick and scream when her temperature is taken?
- Does my child get excited by praise and jump, laugh, or yell with pleasure?
- Does my child fuss and protest when she is being dressed and having clothing pulled over her head?
- If my child doesn't like a new food, does she make a face and spit it out?
- If my child doesn't get what she wants, does she usually cry or stamp her feet in frustration?
- Does my child seem to express her feelings more loudly than other children her age?
- Am I sometimes embarassed when my child cries, screams, or has an outburst in a public place?

If your responses to many of these questions were "yes" or "most of the time," then your child is probably intense in her reactions. If you responded "no" or "rarely," then your child is probably mild in her reactions. Keep in mind that many two-year-olds are neither very intense nor very mild, but they seem intense because of their developmental stage. What characterizes intensity as a temperamental quality is that parents feel that their child's strong reactions have always been this way rather than being a new behavior.

If your child is very intense, you will have to learn to stay calm when she is in a volatile or explosive mood. Should you try to make her stop her outpouring of feelings, she may intensify her outburst. However, you can take her into another room or off by herself to give her space and time to work through her feelings. At two, she is old enough to understand that her shrieks or screams can be disturbing to other children or adults. An intense child can learn that when she gets carried away with her feelings she needs to be in a private spot so that her behavior doesn't cause problems for others. You can explain to your child, "Sometimes when you get upset, you get very loud. It's okay to be loud, but we have to find a way that you can be loud without bothering other people. If you need to scream, I'll take you to your room until you feel calmer." It's important to help an intense two-year-old to understand that you accept her feelings but that you are setting limits on the way she expresses them. As she gets older, you will be able to help her use words to let you know when she is overwhelmed. If you see your child holding in an outburst, or leaving the room when she is upset, be sure to praise her for not losing her temper. An intense child has to work hard to manage her emotions, and supportive parents can help her to master that skill.

If your child is very mild, she will not be as loud or demanding as other two-year-olds. Although you may enjoy her quiet demeanor, you may also need to help her to use words when she needs help or attention. For example, if you see her looking slightly sad after another child takes a toy from her, you can try saying, "You can say 'That's my ball' if you want." Let her know that she can choose to express herself more strongly, if she wants, but don't push her to become more assertive. Over time, she will develop her own style, consistent with her mild temperament.

17

QUALITY OF MOOD

Some two-year-olds seem to be smiling most of the time. They are usually cheerful and agreeable and seem to be in a good mood. Other two-year-olds appear more serious and seem to smile only when they are particularly pleased or if they think that something is funny. A few two-year-olds frown a lot, and seem to be rather grumpy. Even though all two-year-olds will be happy, serious, sad, or angry at times, a child who *usually* acts a certain way is said to have the temperamental quality of mood that can be described as positive, negative, or somewhere in between.

Like most temperamental qualities, quality of mood can be observed in children even during infancy. If you look at pictures of your child from the past two years, you will probably notice that he has a characteristic expression, and that "look" will give you a clue to his usual quality of mood. (If your child has had frequent illnesses, you can expect that his mood often will be more serious or negative when he is not feeling well. In fact, you may have noticed that you can tell if he is getting sick when you see a shift from his usual mood.)

Most parents, after some reflection, can determine whether their child's usual quality of mood is positive, negative, or somewhere in between. Here are some questions you can answer about your own child to help you make that determination:

76

- When my child wakes up in the morning, does he usually smile and laugh or is he usually complaining or crying?
- When my child sees a new toy, does he smile or frown when he examines it?
- When my child bumps or hurts himself slightly, does he ignore it or does he cry and fuss?
- When my child plays alone, does he seem to be smiling, serious, or frowning most of the time?
- Does my child seem to be in a good mood most of the time, or does he have many days when he seems distressed and fussy much of the time?
- Does my child sometimes act grumpy or cranky at an activity but later tell me or someone else that he had a good time?
- Does my child seem so cheerful most of the time that when he looks unhappy I know that he is really troubled?

If your answers indicate that your two-year-old has a generally positive quality of mood, relax and continue to enjoy your time together! Do be sure, however, to allow your child to act sad or angry when he feels that way. Some parents of cheerful children will always "jolly" them out of their bad moods. Although the parents are often successful, their children may begin to feel as though their parents only want them to act happy, even when they need sympathy.

If you think that your child has a generally negative quality of mood, you may have found that there are days when you are both grouchy much of the time. Even if you are a positive person, a two-year-old's negative mood can hang over you like a cloud all day. You may be trying to figure out a way to cheer your child up, or to fix things so that he won't complain. However, if this negative or serious mood is part of his temperament, all of your efforts may be unsuccessful. You will have a much easier time of it if you can accept that his mood is just part of who he is, and that it's not your fault if he doesn't laugh or smile a lot. You don't have to assume that he is unhappy, since he is likely to maintain the same mood even when he is content. In fact, you can assume that when you see your child smiling or laughing he is enjoying himself enormously, since this is such a change from his usual reaction.

18

PERSISTENCE AND ATTENTION SPAN

Two-year-old children vary in the temperamental quality of persistence and attention span. This quality refers to the length of time for which a child can continue with one activity without needing or wanting to stop. For most two-year-olds, their attention span will depend on the particular activity in which they are engaged. However, some parents observe that their two-year-olds seem to be able to stay involved in a single activity for a long time compared to other children the same age. Other parents notice that their children seem to be interested in moving from one activity to another much more frequently than other children.

The two-year-old with a short attention span is often curious and is interested in many different things. She can be convinced easily to stop one activity and begin another. Parents will enjoy her ability to be flexible in her choice of play, and they will also welcome how easy it is to disengage her from misbehavior by providing her with a more acceptable alternative activity. The child with a short attention span often finds it easy to make transitions, because she is eager to try something new and different.

The two-year-old who is persistent will concentrate on a single toy or activity for a relatively long time. As long as she is playing happily, you will probably enjoy her ability to focus her attention. However, if your child is persisting in an activity that is not acceptable to you, you may not appreciate her ability to stay "on track" quite as much! Persistent children don't like to give up, and when the challenge is to resist bedtime or to refuse to put away toys, you may value this particular temperamental quality less.

These questions will help you to decide whether your child is persistent and has a long attention span compared to other two-year-olds:

- When my child is playing a game with me, does she stay involved for more than five minutes?
- When my child is playing with a favorite toy, will she continue playing with it for ten minutes?
- If my child is given a new toy, can she play with it for 30 minutes before losing interest?
- Will my child return to an activity she has been enjoying if she is interrupted by something else?
- Will my child often refuse to stop an activity even when I want her to do something she enjoys very much?
- If my child is working on a puzzle or a new task, will she stay with it even if it is difficult for her?

If you found that you answered many of the above questions with "yes" or "most of the time," then your child is more persistent than the average two-year-old. If your answers were mostly "no," then your child is probably less persistent than average. However, since the typical two-year-old has a fairly short attention span, you may not know for sure at this point what your child will be like in years to come.

If you feel that your child's attention span is short, you may want to use some of the suggestions in the Key "Demanding Attention" to help her to concentrate longer. However, you can expect that as she gets older, she will gradually develop the ability to persist in an activity for longer than she is able to at this time.

If you can see already that your child is persistent, you will understand better her ability to resist you when you want her to cooperate or make a transition. Persistence, like many temperamental qualities, has advantages and disadvantages. You will be happy when she persists in play when you are busy, and unhappy when she persists in play and you want her to stop! Keep in mind that the persistent two-year-old will in later years be able to use this quality to stick with a task that others may feel is too hard. The same quality that may occasionally make your life as a parent difficult right now can be an asset to her when she grows up.

19

DISTRACTIBILITY

S ome two-year-olds can be distracted easily from an activity, whereas others can tune out most interruptions. The degree to which your two-year-old is distractible or nondistractible is described by this temperamental quality.

If your two-year-old is highly distractible, you have probably noticed that you can interrupt him when he crying by telling him a funny story or showing him a toy. When he is in the midst of misbehaving you can often redirect his interest into an acceptable activity. Should he protest when you are dressing him, you can usually gain his cooperation by entertaining him with a game or song.

If your child is nondistractible, he will resist your efforts to redirect his attention. When he is engaged in playing with one toy and you try to substitute another, he will probably refuse. When he is absorbed in an activity, he will ignore anything you say to him and may even tune out other children's efforts to play with him.

These questions will help you to determine your child's degree of distractibility.

- When my child is playing, does he look up if the doorbell or telephone rings?
- Will my child continue to look at a picture book with me when there are distracting noises, such as car horns or doors slamming?

- If my child is playing in the park, does he look up every time someone passes by?
- If my child is crying, can I distract him by singing or talking to him?
- If my child is playing with a forbidden object, can I substitute an acceptable toy without him objecting?

If your two-year-old is highly nondistractible, you have probably noticed that he is very easy to manage when he is engaged in an activity he enjoys. He can play with just one or two toys at a time and doesn't wander restlessly from toy to toy. If he is also persistent, with a long attention span, you often may find that he can stay pleasantly occupied while you get your own work done. When you want to read a story to him or play a game with him, he stays involved and interested, even if there are interruptions. Of course, you probably have noticed that when you would like to distract your child, it isn't easy to do. If he wants to play with his friend's red truck, your offering him his own blue one won't do. When he is playing happily in the bath, he's likely to ignore the water getting cold and your efforts to get him out.

To get his attention, you will often have to speak louder and more firmly to a nondistractible child to get his attention than you would to a more distractible child. Make sure that when you want his attention you are close to him and looking him in the eye before you speak. If you don't make eye contact, you can assume that he hasn't heard you at all. If you feel as though he doesn't listen, try not to get in the habit of nagging, because he'll respond by tuning you out even more. Instead, use devices such as ringing a bell or clapping your hands when you want his attention, and wait until he looks up before you speak.

If your child is highly distractible, try to notice the kinds of situations that seem to be most distracting to him.

A distractible child often is able to stay focussed when there is less background noise and stimulation. Once he is engaged in an activity, try not to interrupt him. He may play better with just one child than in a group, and do better in a group if the activities are structured and he is not presented with too many choices. In choosing a preschool or childcare, you will want to find a setting that is relatively peaceful so that your child will not be constantly overwhelmed with distracting stimulation.

It is interesting that many parents of distractible children find that their child is able to focus for long periods on television shows or video games. These electronic media seem temporarily to override the child's otherwise distractible temperament, perhaps because the images on the screen change and cause the child to refocus his attention. However, distractible children do not seem to improve their concentration in other areas by spending time in front of a television or video screen. In fact, some parents find that when the show or game is over, their child's behavior seems more distractible.

It is often easy to manage a distractible child's misbehavior by offering him attractive alternatives. If you are creative, you may be able to stay one step ahead of your child by redirecting him rather than by having to say "no." However, even the most creative parents will eventually run out of ways to distract their child, so you might as well say "no" when it is necessary.

Occasionally, the parents of a highly distractible child will feel as though they are living with a little whirlwind, especially if their child is very active as well. The child may even be labelled as "hyperactive," although it is difficult to make that kind of an assessment of a two-year-old. However, if your child has the kind of behavior that makes

84

you wonder whether he is spiralling out of control, be sure to consult your health care provider. If your child's activity level and distractibility are unusually high, you will be able to get practical suggestions for modifying and controlling his behavior so that you can enjoy your time together more.

20

‚‚‚

SENSITIVITY

A child who seems to be very fussy and particular about small details is often a temperamentally sensitive child. A child with a low threshold of sensitivity notices small differences in the ways that things look, sound, feel, smell, or taste. Because she notices these things, she responds to them more than other children.

If your child has a low threshold of sensitivity, she will surprise you with her keen perceptions. If you change an ingredient in a recipe, she can taste the difference. If you want her to wear a shirt that she feels doesn't look right with her pants, she'll object. If her socks are inside out, she'll complain, and if her waistband is too tight, she'll refuse to wear her skirt. A sensitive child will notice your moods, or the expression on your face, and may ask you if you're angry when you haven't said anything at all! A sensitive child often has an excellent memory for pictures she's seen or places she has visited because she notices and remembers details.

A child with a high threshold of sensitivity, on the other hand, is much less discriminating about her food and clothing. She doesn't seem to notice people or things as precisely. She may notice when something is different, but she doesn't seem bothered by small changes. She is observant, but isn't as tuned-in to details as the sensitive child.

These questions will help you decide the degree to which your child has a high or low threshold of sensitivity:

- Does my child notice if I mix a small amount of food she dislikes in with food she enjoys?
- Does my child notice if I change the brand or type of milk or juice?
- Does my child notice and react to odors such as perfume or smoke?
- Does my child like to wash her hands when they are dirty?
- Does my child notice small details in book illustrations?
- Does my child object to wearing clothing that isn't soft or that feels a little tight?

If you answer many of these questions "yes," your child probably has a lower threshold of sensitivity than other two-year-olds. If your answers were mostly "no," than your child probably has a higher threshold of sensitivity than other children her age. Of course, some children are very sensitive and particular in certain areas, and less so in others. However, if your child's area of sensitivity seems to be persistent over time, it is likely that this is truly a temperamental quality, not just fickle childhood taste.

If your child does seem extremely sensitive, try to respect her feelings about the details of life that are important to her. If she has favorite foods or clothing, you may find it easier and more practical to offer her a menu and a wardrobe that she prefers. If she hates to wear a starched dress, let her wear a cotton T-shirt. If she can't stand the smell of garlic, leave it out of the spaghetti sauce. As she gets older, she can learn that there are times when you have to be polite and wear or eat things you'd prefer to avoid, but a two-year-old can't understand that idea! If you get very frustrated, keep in mind that the sensitive and discriminating two-year-old often becomes an adult with interesting and perceptive tastes.

If your two-year-old has a high threshold of sensitivity, she is probably very easy to manage. Meals and clothing are easy to plan, and she won't be bothered by changes in the way a sensitive child is bothered. This easygoing quality has disadvantages at times. The less sensitive two-year-old won't notice or care that she has dirt on her face and paint all over her dress, or that she's left muddy footprints all over the kitchen floor!

Part Three

〜〜

TYPICAL TWO-YEAR-OLD BEHAVIOR AND MISBEHAVIOR

I f you are parents of a two-year-old, you know that your child often behaves in ways that would be *mis*behaving if he were an older child. One of the biggest challenges for parents of two-year-olds is deciding what behavior to accept, what behavior to ignore, and what behavior you should try to change. In the Keys that follow, you'll read about many different types of two-year-old behavior and misbehavior, and suggestions for how you can respond.

As you read these Keys, you will probably recognize some behavior that you're seeing in your child right now, and other behavior that doesn't seem typical at all. Every child is different. There probably have been times when you have watched other two-year-olds and wondered why they behave so much better (or worse) than your child. Of course, their parents may have been looking at your child and thinking the same thing! Spending time with other two-year-olds and their parents talking about the differences you notice can be a wonderful way to help you appreciate your child and learn more about parenting. These Keys can be a guide to the range of behavior you'll see, but the best guide will be your own observations of your child and other children his age.

21

GETTING ALONG WITH PARENTS

As a two-year-old becomes more independent, his relationship with his parents changes. There is no predictable pattern or timing for these changes, but they are a result of your child's trying to find out more about how he is different from you. Much of your child's energy this year will be devoted to figuring out how to "become himself." He will often experiment with being a person just like his parents by imitating what you do: trying on your clothes, working around the house, talking in your tone of voice, or "playing parent" in an imaginary game with his playmates or the family pet. He may become your "shadow," staying close to you and wanting to be involved in everything you do.

Sometimes a child will show a strong preference for one parent over the other as he sorts out who he wants to be. He may cling to Mom and push Dad away, or he may act as though Mom is a second-class citizen compared to Dad. It can be hard on either parent when this occurs. If your two-year-old is always wanting Mommy to care for him and refusing Dad's involvement, Mom may start to feel overburdened. At the same time, she may find it hard to resist her toddler calling for her help or comfort, especially if the child gets upset when Dad tries to help. Other two-year-olds will start to prefer Dad to Mom, and push away their mother's efforts to care for them or play with them. If

Mom has been the primary caregiving parent, she may feel as though all of her hard work in the early years is now unappreciated. If she is working outside the home, she may worry that her child doesn't want her because she has been away all day. Most mothers and fathers find this kind of rejection very painful.

Even though a parent naturally feels hurt when a child prefers the other parent, it's important to recognize this behavior as a phase of your child's normal development. If you get upset with your child for preferring the other parent, he may react by intensifying his preference. If you make the issue of "who does what" a power struggle in your family, your two-year-old is likely to win by becoming angry and resistant.

The best approach to take is to accept that when both parents are present, the "preferred parent" will be more active and the other parent will be helpful in any way that he or she can. At the same time, the "preferred parent" should make an effort to leave the child alone with the other parent on a regular basis, even if the child protests. In this way, the child and the parent who is being pushed away will have time to work out a good relationship. Parents who use this approach find that their two-year-olds adapt very quickly once the choice of parents is removed. Of course, once the "preferred parent" returns, the child may act as though he is being rescued from a desert island, even though he has been having a great time up until that moment!

A common problem that arises during this year of a child's life is a lack of time. Most parents are so busy with responsibilities beyond caring for their child that it is easy for them to become overwhelmed with work. When parents are tired or under stress they often cut corners on the time

91

they spend with their young children. They may use more baby-sitters or leave their child later in daycare, or they may spend more time at home talking on the telephone or trying to get housework done. They may tell a child that they are going to a park, but wind up doing several errands on the way. Unfortunately, a two-year-old will not be sympathetic to his parents' needs to do other activities. Although he is old enough to learn to wait for short periods for attention, if he feels that his parents are too busy to make time for him, he will react negatively. Depending on his personality and temperamental style, this negative reaction may be provocative, angry, or quietly resigned. For example, he may misbehave whenever you are ready to go to work, or whenever you try to get him to hurry. He may seem to go along with your fast pace until he gets overtired himself, and then have a tantrum "for no reason." He may refuse to go to bed at night, prolonging his bedtime routine in an effort to get you to spend more time with him. A child who is missing his parents can become so demanding of attention that his parents may begin to give him *less* time because their time together has become unpleasant.

Parents who feel that their lives are sometimes too busy should take a moment to add up the hours in a day spent on all of their different activities: working, sleeping, cooking, cleaning, shopping, commuting, and the routine tasks of childcare. Is there time on a daily basis for your child to get your undivided attention, just for fun and play? When you are with your child are you usually able to give him your full attention or are you often distracted? If you look at your daily life from your child's point of view, do you think that he knows that you really enjoy his company? Your answers to these questions may cause you to reconsider the way you are spending your time. Sometimes tasks that seem important aren't really as critical as we think. A parent who decided to make more time for her young daughter said, "I realized that my last words were not going to be, 'I wish I'd spent more time at the office.'"

As you and your spouse examine your schedules to look at the time you spend with your child, you both also need to look at the amount of time you spend alone with each other. It may seem contradictory, but as much as your child needs you to spend time with him, he also needs to see you having time with each other. He's learning about what it means to have a partner, and how married people treat each other. If he only sees you as his parents, he's only learning about one part of your family life. Keeping your couple relationship healthy takes time, but it's worth figuring out a way to do it. Some couples have a "date" once a week, others squeak by on once a month. See if you can find a regular sitter, or perhaps trade childcare with another couple on alternate Saturday nights. If your two-year-old learns to look forward to these trades, you may be able to expand to overnight visits, and you and your partner can have a second honeymoon!

22

~~~~~~

GETTING ALONG WITH OTHER CHILDREN

T wo-year-old children usually enjoy the company of other children. However, because normal two-year-olds are involved with themselves and their own needs and interests, their style of play is different from that of older children. Parents sometimes worry that their two-year-old's self-centeredness is a barrier to making friends, not realizing that this characteristic is typical of this age group. A commonly voiced concern of parents is, "If my child acts this way, no one will want to play with him when he gets older." Fortunately, the self-centeredness of this age gradually gives way to more sociability as a child matures, especially if parents provide opportunities for the child to play with other children and practice having fun in small groups.

A two-year-old will like being with a companion who is fun to watch and pleasant to be around, but he will not care about "being nice" in order to help the other child have a good time. That means he is unlikely to want to share his toys or include another child in his activity if he feels that means he has to give up some of his own pleasure. As a parent, you may feel that your two-year-old is acting selfishly. He's not. He's acting like a two-year-old!

Two-year-olds often play next to each other, each child directing his own activity, talking to himself, and making decisions about what he wants to do next. Sometimes two-year-olds will talk to each other, and sometimes they will build on each other's play for a few minutes. But you generally will not see two-year-olds playing interactively in the kind of imaginary or structured games in which three-year-olds engage. This characteristic of two-year-old play is usually described as "parallel play," but the word parallel implies that the children never join up in their activiites. In fact, two-year-olds may be able to interact quite well as long as neither one feels as though he has to give up something he wants in order to please the other one!

Since most children this age lack the skills of sharing, taking turns, letting another child have his way, or resolving disagreements with words, parents need to stay closely involved when their two-year-olds are playing with each other. Every time your child plays with another child he learns something about getting along with others. If you are close by, you can watch for the moment when two children are struggling over the same toy, or one child has his hand raised ready to whack the other one. At that moment, you can step in to distract or redirect the children, to help them to solve the problem with words, or to remind them about being gentle. In this way, you're modelling and teaching the kind of behavior you want your child to be learning. If you aren't close by, you won't see problems building until they've led to tears, arguments, or a hurt child. At that point, your choice will be to reprimand or comfort the children and they will have missed a chance to learn how to solve a problem without creating a conflict.

Two-year-olds will often play best with older children. An older child is often—but not always—tolerant of the younger child's limited skills and vocabulary. An older child also enjoys being able to boss a younger child around, and a two-year-old will usually cooperate to get attention! However, the older child, especially if he is a sibling, will probably not be tolerant of your two-year-old's behavior if he becomes too provocative or negative, so you will have to supervise this relationship as well.

A two-year-old's most difficult relationship occurs when he is with a baby or younger toddler. A two-year-old is too young to understand how a child younger or smaller than he is needs to be treated. He has very poor impulse control, and if the younger child bothers him, he can push or hit in a way that can cause serious harm. Even if he is trying to be helpful, a two-year-old can underestimate his own ability. One child was upset about his baby sister's crying, so he pulled a chair over to her crib and tried to lift her out to carry her in to his mother! The potential for danger is too great when a two-year-old is alone with a younger child, so an adult needs to be close by at all times.

Two-year-olds, despite their lack of social skills, can enjoy small group activities very much. You may find that a play group or a parent-involvement toddler program is an ideal way to meet other parents and offer your child an opportunity to be entertained and stimulated by other children. If you are leaving your child in a small group, be sure that there are enough adults to supervise the children closely. Remember that the closer the supervision, the more likely it is that the adults can work to prevent problems, rather than reacting to them *after* they occur.

In many communities, birthday parties for two- and three-year-olds have become popular social events, perhaps because they seem to be a good way to bring children and parents together for a weekend activity. Unfortunately, for many two-year-olds, big, busy parties are overwhelming. Most two-year-olds will enjoy a quiet party with a few activities in a familiar setting. Some two-year-olds will seem to love the excitement of a big birthday party but will be exhausted and cranky for the rest of the day. A few two-year-olds will arrive at a party and begin to misbehave, perhaps by running about out of control, or perhaps by hitting or shoving other children. If your child loves parties and behaves nicely both during and after, then there's no reason to modify your social schedule. But if you notice that the parties tend to cause your child to act up, either at the party or later in the day, you may want to skip these social events until he's older. Two-year-olds are challenged enough when they try to get along with one playmate, and asking them to be a social butterfly at this age is often asking for trouble!

23

DEMANDING ATTENTION

"**M**y two-year-old needs me to entertain her all the time! When will she learn to play by herself?" Most parents of two-year-olds wonder if the time will ever come when they can finish a telephone call, take a shower, or even read the newspaper without being interrupted by their child wanting to play. Toy catalogues promise that your child will have "hours of fun" with some colorful, expensive, educational something-or-other, but they don't tell you that the hours will probably be spread out in three minute bits over the next year or so! The average two-year-old can't play alone for long, although some two-year-olds manage better than others. Some of the differences among children are due to the temperamental factors described in Part Two of this book. Other differences in the length of time a child can play alone are a result of how parents teach a child to enjoy her own company.

If you feel that your two-year-old has difficulty playing alone, take some time to observe her pattern and style of play at home and in other settings. The child who is persistent and not easily distracted will be able to play alone longer than the child whose attention span is shorter. Sometimes a parent can help a child learn to stay involved with an activity by gently refocussing her attention. For example, if your child tends to pick up a toy, play with it for thirty seconds, and throw it aside, try sitting with the toy yourself and showing her different things that she can do with it. If she still moves on to another activity, you don't have to follow her lead. Rather, you can continue to stay where you are and wait for your child to return to you. In this way, you are showing your child that it is possible to stay interested in one activity for a few minutes, even though you aren't forcing her to do so. You are also showing her that you can be with her without having to play with her. If you follow your child around the room, switching your activity whenever she does, she'll enjoy herself but you will tire quickly and your child will continue to expect you to follow her until you drop!

Sometimes a two-year-old is sociable by nature and enjoys playing with anyone, whether the playmate is a parent, a sibling, another child, or a baby-sitter. A child with this kind of personality needs companionship, and it may be hard for a parent to keep up with her demands all day. She's not old enough for you to let her play with a friend without constant supervison, but you can try to arrange play dates where you and another parent watch each other's children for a few hours. You may find that it is less work to watch two two-year-olds than one, and you'll also get some time off.

Sometimes a child feels that if she doesn't demand her parent's attention she won't get it. It's easy to give her attention only when she asks for it, and ignore her when she's quiet. Although this response makes sense from a tired parent's point of view, the child is rewarded for just the kind of behavior you want to discourage!

To turn this pattern around, a parent can begin by frequently initiating play with their child before she has a chance to demand your attention. Set aside at least five minutes to play with your child, doing anything that you both enjoy. Tell your child that you have time to play now, until it's time for you to make breakfast, change your clothes, or do some other task that your child can understand as part of your daily routine. Play with your child, giving her your full attention. Then tell her, "I have to go make breakfast now. We'll play again later." If your child wants to join in your next activity, let her, but end the playtime even if she protests. Take care of the task you said you were going to perform, and then tell your child, "Now I can play with you again." Keep offering your child your full attention for her play, but end the playtime yourself. If you keep the playtimes and your own activity times short, your child won't have to wait too long for you. Although at first this kind of structured play will feel more time consuming, over time your child will learn to accept your coming and going.

Most parents of two-year-olds will find themselves turning on the "electronic baby-sitter"—the television set—as a way of coping with their child's need for entertainment. There's no evidence that the television programs for young children shown on the noncommercial channels are harmful. In fact, most child development experts feel that programs such as "Mister Rogers" and "Sesame Street" help expose children to music, storytelling, and information that enhances their learning. Many two-year-olds watch one to two hours of these shows daily. If your child is watching television, however, you should be aware of some of the problems that are associated with the "TV habit."

Some children will watch television quietly for hours at a time. Then, when the parent turns the TV off, they seem to be irritable, cranky, or demanding. If this is the case with your child, you may need to reduce the amount of time she spends in front of the set. Other children seem fine when they watch shows designed for young children, but are upset by cartoons, live shows, and commercials that are aimed towards older children and adults. A two-year-old has difficulty understanding that what she sees on TV isn't real. The stories and action on many television shows include scenes of strong emotions or violence that can be extremely confusing or frightening for her. In addition, many television shows also include commercials for the news or for other programming that highlight scary or life threatening events that have happened to other people, including children. It's not unusual for a child who watches these programs to have nightmares or to start being afraid when her parents leave her. Even if your two-year-old doesn't seem upset by what she sees on television, she still may be absorbing more thoughts and impressions about the world than you would like. So take a careful look at what your child is watching before you use TV to give yourself a needed break.

Even if you have a two-year-old who plays by herself at times, takes a long nap, and enjoys watching educational TV, you are still going to find it hard to amuse her by yourself every day. She is at the age where her curiosity and need for stimulation would exceed the patience of most parents. Try to get some relief for yourself and diversion for her by going with her to a park, to an organized play group, or by having a sitter come into your home. Some parents have a young school-age child come over and play with their two-year-old several afternoons a week. The older child may be too young to take care of your child independently, but he can amuse your toddler while you get some time to yourself. If you are refreshed, your child's continued demands for your attention will be easier for you to handle.

24

~~~~~~

COMMUNICATING WITH YOUR TWO-YEAR-OLD

A s your two-year-old has more thoughts and feelings to share with you, and as you expect him to understand more and more of what's on your mind, you will want to build good communication skills for now and the years to come. Communication is more than talking. Communication includes listening to another person's words, and trying to understand his feelings. This kind of listening helps the other person to feel good about letting you know more about himself.

Parents of young children often complain, "When I talk to Jimmy, he acts as though he hasn't heard anything I say." It's true that children sometimes ignore what grown-ups say, or at least act as if they are ignoring them. Of course, many times grown-ups seem to ignore what children are saying, or at least act that way. An effective way of helping a child to pay attention to you when you talk is to pay attention to him when he talks to you. When you are talking and listening to your child, try to:

- Make eye contact when he is speaking. Look at him while he talks, even if you can hear what he is saying without looking at him.
- When you cannot look at your child because you are driving or doing a task that requires you to watch what you're doing, tell your child, "I'm listening, but I can't look at you right now. But I can hear your words."

- Whenever you can, move to your child's level to talk and listen, either by kneeling down or by bringing him up high enough to make good eye contact. If you are telling your child something important, try putting your hand on his shoulder or knee to get his attention focussed on you.
- While your child is talking, lean forward a little and show him by your facial expression that you are interested in his words. Encourage him to continue with expressions like, "Mm-hmm," "Go on," or "Tell me more about that."

A great deal of communication involves simple exchanges of information: "Where are your shoes?" "In the hall, I think." "Let's find them so we can go out." However, even simple exchanges can often include feelings: "Where have you put your shoes now?" "In the hall, I think." "Why can't you ever put your shoes where they belong?" You can see how different words and tones can change the nature of the communication between parent and child. Children notice, and react to, our feelings as well as our words. By being aware of our children's feelings when they talk, we can become more aware of the way in which we express ourselves to them.

You can perceive your child's feelings as well as his words by using the technique of *reflective listening*. Reflective listening is like holding a mirror up to your child when he talks, with your words being the mirror of his feelings. A two-year-old often cannot put his feelings into words without help. If you pay attention to how he expresses himself and offer him words that seem to fit what he is feeling, you show him that you care about what he wants to tell you. At the same time you will be teaching him the words that he can eventually use to express himself better.

For example, if your child is rubbing his eyes while you are coming home from the park, you can say, "You feel tired from playing so hard." If he is bubbling over with words about something he has seen, you can say, "You're really excited about seeing that fire engine!" If he is crying because another child took his toy, try "You feel sad because Jeff took your shovel." If he refuses to put on his jacket to go home, you can say, "You're angry because you don't want to leave right now."

Reflective listening can also help solve problems. When Joey's Mom was sick, she had to stay in bed. Joey kept banging on the door of her bedroom, even though his Dad explained to him many times that Mommy needed to rest and that Joey couldn't go in. Joey kept saying, "I want Mommy! I don't want you!" Finally, his Dad reflected Joey's feelings back to him: "You're angry that you can't see Mommy. You're sad that she can't play with you. You miss your Mommy." Joey looked at his Dad, nodded, and went into the other room to play with a favorite toy. Reflective listening will not always make a child feel better right away, but a child will learn that his parents understand and care about his feelings.

Parents also can help children to communicate better if they give positive, rather than negative, messages. A two-year-old will listen better if he doesn't hear a lot of negative messages that make him feel bad about himself.

- When your child misbehaves, try to redirect him rather than scold him. It's better to tell a child what you want him to do instead of telling him only what you don't want him to do. For example, when your two-year-old is shouting, instead of saying "No shouting," you can say, "Shouting is for playing outside. Please use your indoor voice instead." If a child breaks a rule, you can say,

"Remember, the rule is that we walk when we are in the store." Of course, no parent is likely to get through a day without ever saying "No!" but using the word no selectively will help your child pay more attention when you do use it.

- Avoid placing labels on your child that make him think that you *expect* him to misbehave. If your child spills his milk and you say, "Why are you always so clumsy?" he'll feel bad, but he won't learn anything from his mistake except that he must be the kind of child who spills milk a lot. If you say, "Oops, there goes the milk. Here, you wipe the table while I get the floor," he'll learn that you expect him to clean up after his mistakes, but that you don't blame him for making them.

- When you are feeling angry, happy, disappointed, excited, tired, or sad, tell your child how you feel, with a simple explanation of why. By helping your child to understand your feelings, he learns to be more aware that other people have feelings, too. It will be several years before he is able to think of other people's feelings as being as important as his own, but this is the time to start giving him the words to talk about them. You can explain difficult feelings by saying, "I'm angry because you hit me when I was putting your shoes on you" or "I'm sad because I lost my book at the beach." A short explanation is usually satisfying to a two-year-old.

As you think about communicating with your two-year-old, remember that he is always listening as his parents talk to each other. If he hears you showing warmth and respect in the way you communicate, he will model what he hears. If you feel that your adult communication patterns could use some improvement, now is the time to work on them, so your two-year-old will learn the best possible skills from you.

25

TEMPER TANTRUMS

I f your two-year-old has not had a temper tantrum yet, he is quite likely to have one, and probably more than one, sometime this year. A temper tantrum is a child's way of expressing anger and frustration at a time when he is feeling out of control. Your child may yell, shriek, or scream. He may run around in circles, throw himself on the floor, or lash out at you by hitting, kicking, or throwing things. Some children have silent or sulky tantrums, refusing to talk or make eye contact. Others make so much noise that parents worry that the neighbors will call the police! No matter how your child behaves during a tantrum, if you are like most parents you will probably feel very helpless as you watch your child erupt in fury. You may have feelings of failure or incompetence as a parent, or you may be furious at your child for behaving so outrageously. If you're out in public, you may feel as though other people are judging you and your child (they probably are!). It takes a great deal of parental self-confidence to handle a two-year-old's tantrums successfully, and the information in this Key will help you keep your head when your child seems to be losing his!

Even though tantrums are common and even predictable among two-year-olds, most parents wonder if the tantrums are a reflection on their own parenting ability. They are *not*! Tantrums are simply a part of life with a young child. Although you cannot prevent your child from having tantrums altogether, you can help him to have fewer tantrums, or to get through his tantrums more quickly. If you understand the causes of your two-year-old's tantrums, you will react better when he is spinning out of control.

The most common cause for a two-year-old to have a tantrum is in response to his parents saying "No." As your toddler becomes more capable and competent, he wants to have more control over his life. By now, he has learned that a good way to get what he wants is to ask for it. It will take him years to accept that even though he asks, your answer sometimes will be "No!" At his age, he can't see your point of view very well. He can't understand why you are refusing to give him what he wants and so he gets angry. He doesn't understand these angry feelings, and he hasn't learned to control them yet, so he has a tantrum.

A two-year-old may also have tantrums when he is unable to tell his parents or another person what he is thinking. A two-year-old can talk, but his ability to express himself in words is not as advanced as his ability to think. He understands much more than he can say. When he knows what he wants to say but can't say it, he will feel angry with himself *and* angry at you for not being able to understand him! Many parents find that as their two-year-old learns to use more and more words to express himself, his tantrums decrease. In fact, one of the best ways for parents to help children learn to control their anger is by being good models themselves. If you are the kind of parent—and many of us are, at times—who kicks the furniture or storms about when you lose your temper, you should practice using the phrase, "I'm angry right now" so that your child will learn that there are words that people can use to express these feelings.

Most parents would like to be able to prevent all temper tantrums, but that's not possible. However, if your child is having tantrums every day or many times a week, you may be able to observe some patterns that will help you to decrease the number of tantrums, even if you can't eliminate them entirely. Watch your child for several days, perhaps even taking notes, to see what you can observe about when, where, and under what circumstances the tantrums occur.

Some two-year-olds have tantrums when they are overtired. Many parents learn that if their child misses his nap, stays up too late, or awakens too early, they can expect a tantrum. Other two-year-olds have tantrums when they are overstimulated. They may have a wonderful time at a birthday party or on a family outing, but when they come home they fall apart and have a tantrum. Other children have a temper tantrum when they have to make a transition from one activity to another. They don't want to stop what they are doing, and they get furious at having someone interrupt them. All these situations are likely to occur in the course of normal life with a toddler, and it's unlikely that you can avoid them entirely.

One pattern of tantrum behavior that often can be controlled is the tantrum that occurs in the hungry two-year-old. Many children in this age group are so busy playing that they don't notice that they are hungry. Some parents notice that their child starts to get short-tempered or fragile if he goes more than a few hours without a snack, and that a tantrum can be avoided by offering food. Some children also seem to be especially irritable after they have eaten certain foods, especially processed or high sugar foods or foods with chemical additives. Research on the relationship between these foods and children's behavior is not conclusive, but if a parent notices a clear pattern of behavior in response to diet, these foods should be avoided.

If you can predict the situations that are likely to cause your child to have a tantrum, you may be able to avoid or minimize problems. If you know your child is overtired or has been on his "best behavior" for longer than usual, you can take a quiet time-out for the two of you to wind down. You may start to notice some early signs that your child is reaching his limit and is ready for a tantrum. If you can catch him before he loses control completely, you may be able to help him by expressing his feelings in words for him. For example, if you see your child getting frustrated with a toy that he can't make work in the way he would like, you might sit down next to him and say, "You're really having a hard time with that. It looks like you're getting angry." If your child is exhausted and cranky on the way home from an outing, you can say, "When we get home it might be hard for you to settle in. Maybe we'll sit and read a story while I cuddle you."

However, no matter how careful and observant you are, your child probably will still have some tantrums and you will have to help him deal with his anger without getting caught up in it yourself. The key to managing a temper tantrum once it begins is to stay calm. When your child is out of control, he needs to know that he can count on you to take care of him. If he feels that his anger provokes your anger, he will become even more upset. He may be yelling at you or even trying to hit or kick you, but if you respond to him in the same way he will learn that it's acceptable to act that way. When your child loses control, don't try to make him stop. Instead, stay near him and let him feel that you are there to help. If he pauses for breath, or seems to be continuing to rant for more than a few minutes, you can attempt to comfort him. Some children will welcome a gentle interruption, but others will push you away until they have gotten out their angry feeling on their own.

Once your child calms down, he needs your help to put into words what he has been feeling. By doing this, you can let your child know that you can accept his angry feelings without rejecting him and he will not be so overwhelmed by them. You can say, "You were so upset. You were so angry. You screamed and yelled because you were angry. Now you are quiet." You can also offer your child other ways to get his angry feeling out. "You were so angry you were hitting the table, and you even tried to hit me. Let's find something that you can hit when you're angry that won't get hurt." You can find a pillow or a punching bag that will work better than furniture and people. You can also help your child see that it is okay to be angry, but that it is not okay to hurt you or anyone else. Tell your child, "I won't hurt you when I get angry, and I won't let you hurt me." Of course, to tell your child this and be effective, this statement must be true.

One of the toughest problems parents face with two-year-old tantrums is when the parent says "No" without thinking and their child unexpectedly gets furious. This problem can be especially challenging if the family is out in public and parents are feeling awkward or self-conscious about their child making a scene. Parents often feel that they would have said "Yes" if they had realized how important the matter was to their child. Sometimes they will change their minds in response to the child's anger. Unfortunately, a two-year-old who learns that he can get his parents to change their minds by having a tantrum is likely to learn very quickly to have more tantrums to get his way. Of course, all parents occasionally change their minds, and there are times that even the strictest parents will want to avoid a tantrum. But if you feel that you have fallen into a habit of rethinking your decisions based on how upset your child gets, or if you find that you are giving in to his demands for fear of his having a tantrum, it's a good idea to start saying "No" more often and more consistently. You may have to endure more tantrums for a short while, but if you can stay calm and firm, your child will learn that a tantrum isn't the best way to argue with you or to get your attention!

26

SEPARATION:
LEARNING TO SAY
GOOD-BYE

Throughout this book, you have been reading about your two-year-old's need to assert her independence from you. Her desire to do things for herself, to push you away, and to say "No" even when you know she would like to say "Yes" are some of the ways in which she is separating her identity from yours. The struggle that she is going through internally, between being close to you and venturing out on her own, is not one-sided. As parents, you are probably experiencing conflicting feelings about your child's growing independence. You probably would like to have time away from her, to be free from the ongoing responsibilities for her care, to have time for yourselves as adults, and more time to do the work that you have to do to support your family.

Your two-year-old's need to separate from you and your need to separate from her are opportunities for both child and parents to have a positive experience that can set the foundation for lifelong independence. It's important for your child to find ways to feel sadness about being away from you, but at the same time to feel successful about being independent and happy when she is reunited with you. As parents, you need to learn to feel sad but still allow yourselves to leave your child. Sometimes parents try to protect a child from feeling sad by not leaving her at all: "Emma gets so distressed when we leave her with a sitter that we've just gotten used to taking her everywhere with us." Other parents, perhaps feeling guilty about leaving their child, may minimize their child's negative reaction or not recognize that their child needs help in learning to separate: "Oh, Jenny always carries on like that when we leave, so we've learned to ignore her fuss."

Most two-year-olds have difficulty when their parents leave them. Some children, especially those who have been cared for by other loving adults since infancy, seem to be very comfortable about being left in familiar situations. Even children who adapt quickly and who are used to being away from their parents may, at age two, start to act upset when they are left in a new situation. A two-year-old doesn't say to herself, "Well, I did fine without my Mom and Dad when I was with a sitter, so I should do just fine now that I'm starting nursery school." Nor can a two-year-old be expected to think, "Well, I really liked having Grandma visit me last summer, so I won't be upset if my parents leave me at her house for the weekend." A two-year-old simply cannot make the connections between places and people that adults can make, and a new setting that her parents feel is safe and secure may not feel that way to her at all.

It is hard to know what goes on in a young child's mind when she is feeling sad or frightened because she is separated from her parents. If her parents say good-bye in a way that shows they understand her feelings, if she gets lots of attention and kindness from the people who care for her while they are gone, and if she has a warm reunion when her parents return, she is likely to associate the sadness of separation with positive feelings as well. These experiences form the basis for her feeling that other people can help her when her parents are gone, and that though her parents are gone, they will return and continue to love her.

However, some children are left with people who don't have the time or training to understand and respond to a young child's sadness. A crying child may be ignored or excluded from play. Some parents are too busy or preoccupied to take the time to help their children say good-bye or to give them their full attention when they are reunited. These children may feel that when their parents leave, they are always going to feel sad and lonely and that no one helps them to feel better. As these children get older, they may have difficulty separating from their parents at other times, whether to spend the night at a friend's or to go off to camp.

To help your two-year-old have a more positive experience as she learns to separate from you, try to make sure that her caregivers understand that young children need help in this way. Ask how the caregiver helps children adjust to being left. A teenage sitter will often be as knowledgeable as a trained professional, telling you that she likes to start playing with your two-year-old and making friends with her before you leave, so that the two of them are having fun when Mommy and Daddy have to leave. A teacher may tell you that she always greets a child and parent on arrival to say hello and help them both feel comfortable. Good-bye routines and rituals are helpful for children as a way of starting the day and marking the time of leave-taking from parents, so it's important to allow time in your morning to get your child settled before saying good-bye. Even though it can be tempting to sneak off while your child is playing, it is better for your child to see you leave than to suddenly find that you have "disappeared." If a caregiver does not seem concerned about separation issues or seems to blame parents for worrying too much about their children's feelings, you may want to ask yourself if the attitude expressed is one that is compatible with yours.

Your two-year-old may find it easier to leave you if she has a regular routine with a sitter or play group. If a child is starting full-time care, one of the best ways to assure a smooth adjustment is to start the child in part-time care several weeks earlier. Rather than experiencing a sudden change to her whole daily routine, the child has time to get used to being left and reunited with her parent in gradual doses.

Even if your child is used to being separated from you, it is a good idea to avoid making many different changes in her routine at the same time. For example, if she is starting a new childcare program, it would be better to avoid scheduling a business trip or hosting a group of visitors from out-of-town. Not all disruptions are preventable, of course. If you have a new baby just at the time that your child is ready to start nursery school you can't, and shouldn't, postpone leaving her there. At the same time, you will want to be sure that you try to keep stable as many routines as you can during the time of transition.

Two-year-olds are often helped to adjust to separation by having parents tell them stories about other children whose mommies and daddies leave them with other people. Using stuffed animals, puppets, or just your imagination, you can tell your child the story of another child whose parents have to be away from her. You can talk about the little girl's sad feelings and how the caregivers and other children help her to feel better and have fun during the day. You can have her parents come back and tell her how they missed her and how happy they are to see her. In this way,

115

your child will be able to think about how she will deal with her feelings of missing you and see that you will return and be happy to see her, too.

When your child first begins to spend time away from you, whether it is in someone else's home or in a program for young children, she will need to feel that you are a part of her day even when you aren't there. One way to accomplish this is to take time when you arrive and when you leave to talk to the caregiver. This interaction can be brief, exchanging information about how the day or evening before has gone, but it often helps your child see that you are having a relationship with the caregiver. If she sees that you like the person who takes care of her, she will be more comfortable. When you pick your child up, spend some time looking at any toys or projects she wants to share with you, and say hello to the other children, too. Let your child know that this place where she spends her time is a place that you enjoy visiting and that you think is important.

Sometimes when a parent arrives to pick up their child, the child will act as though she isn't interested in going home or even in saying hello. It can be upsetting to a parent who has hurried to pick her child up to be treated as though she wasn't even missed! When a child behaves this way, it's usually because she needs some time to make the transition back to her parent from the day's activities. Sometimes, a child who has been well behaved in her parents' absence will begin to be disruptive or provocative when the parent arrives. The child does not do this to make a parent feel unloved or angry, although that is often the result of her behavior. Rather, it is the action of a child who has been containing her negative impulses all day and is finally allowing herself to be negative with the person she trusts the most—her parent.

No matter what your child's reaction to seeing you when you return, she will expect your full attention and energy. However, if you're like most parents, you need some time to take care of yourself at the end of a long day of work. Going directly from the demands of your job to the demands of parenthood is asking a lot! If you are tired and frazzled on your way to pick her up, try to take a moment to relax and restore yourself before you greet your child. Even if you're pressed for time, you have needs, too. Some parents take a walk around the block before picking up their child. Others will take deep breaths for a few minutes, or sit quietly with eyes closed, or use other calming exercises that work for them. Five minutes for yourself isn't much, but it can make a big difference in your ability to respond positively to your two-year-old.

Separations can be hard for children and parents, but when parents and caregivers set the stage for loving good-byes and happy reunions, they can be positive learning experiences for everyone in the family.

27

DIFFICULTIES AT BEDTIME AND DURING THE NIGHT

Most two-year-olds occasionally will resist going to bed, falling asleep, or staying asleep. About one-third of two-year-olds awaken during the night and wake their parents up as well. If your two-year-old's difficulties in sleeping at night interfere with your own ability to awaken well-rested in the morning, your family has a sleep problem. If you are the kind of parent who falls asleep quickly at bedtime or after being awakened at 2:00 A.M. your response to your child's sleep patterns will probably be different from the parent who takes an hour to fall asleep at bedtime and after every nighttime interruption. Some parents enjoy having a two-year-old crawl in bed with them at night. Other parents find that they cannot sleep well with a squirmy child next to them, or that having their child in their bed interferes with their relationship as a couple. There's no "right" way for a child or family to sleep. However, this Key will give you some ideas for managing common sleep problems of two-year-olds.

Sleep Association Habits

Everyone has habits that help them to feel comfortable and secure when they fall asleep. For example, most adults like to have the lights turned out, a pillow under their heads, and a blanket pulled over them. If a light is left on, or the pillow or blanket is taken away, it may be hard for the person who has these habits to fall asleep. Children are just like adults in their sleep habits. They get used to falling asleep with a special blanket, a stuffed animal, or perhaps a parent who rocks or holds them while they fall asleep. Some adults can continue to sleep through the night even if the lights are turned on or their bedding is tossed onto the floor, just as some children can stay asleep if their blanket is at the foot of the bed or their parent leaves to sleep in her own room. But some adults and children are so sensitive to their environment that if the comfort habits they require at bedtime are not present when they rouse slightly during the night, they wake up and have to get everything back to "just right." When a two-year-old needs you to help him fall asleep at bedtime and then calls you repeatedly during the night to visit him, hold him, or stay with him, he is letting you know that he has developed a sleep association habit of only being able to fall asleep with you near. Some children sleep through the night but need their parents to stay with them to help them fall asleep at bedtime.

If you feel that your child has this sleep association habit, you can change his pattern by gradually moving away from helping him to fall asleep. Your starting point will be to discontinue holding or rocking or lying next to him, or whatever your customary pattern is now. A first step might be to sit at the foot of his bed, or to put a chair next to his bed and sit there while he falls asleep. Your child will probably object, but if you stay calm and firm, saying no more than, "You're okay, go to sleep now," he will fall asleep. Every few nights, move further away from your child until you are sitting outside his bedroom door. If your child wakes during the night, go to him but stay sitting in the chair just as you did at bedtime. This kind of gradual

119

withdrawal will take a few weeks of hard work, but your child will eventually learn to fall asleep and return to sleep on his own. It is very helpful to keep a "sleep diary" of your child's patterns, beginning about a week before you start the program, so that you can identify patterns and note improvements.

If this kind of program doesn't work for you, you may need to explore your feelings about staying with your child at night. If you feel as though your child's sleep is disrupting your daytime life and you are feeling as though it is hard to solve the problem on your own, talk to your health care provider or a specialist in children's sleep problems.

Nightmares

Nightmares are common among young children. A nightmare is a dream in which something occurs that frightens a child, usually enough to cause him to awaken, crying or calling for help. When you go to your child, he is awake, crying or asking you to hold and comfort him. He may talk about the dream, or use words that let you know that he has been frightened. After you comfort him by letting him know that he has had a "bad dream" and that you are there, he probably will relax and settle down, but he may not want you to leave him. Unless sleeping with your child is very disruptive to your own sleep, there is no harm in letting him spend the rest of the night with you, either in his room or yours. Most children will not develop a night-waking pattern because parents respond in this way to an occasional nightmare. However, if your child is having nightmares several times a week over a period of several weeks, you should look for reasons that might explain why his dreams are so disturbing to him. Sometimes a stressful event will cause a child to have nightmares. A scary television show or story may also stimulate nightmares. At times, a child who is having difficulty with separation from his parents during the day will have nightmares at night. If you keep a record of the pattern of your child's nightmares, you may be able to find a relationhip between his daytime life and his nighttime sleep that can help you to prevent more nightmares.

Night Terrors

A two-year-old who is having a night terror will awaken his parents with the sounds of his crying, screaming, and thrashing about. When his parents rush in to him, he will continue to cry, seemingly unaware of their presence. His eyes may be wide open but he will have a glazed, staring expression. If his parents try to comfort him he will act as though they aren't there or even push them away. If they manage to wake him from his screaming, he will look at them in dazed confusion, because he will have no memory of having been crying. However, if he sees his parents looking at him in horror, for no apparent reason, he may then begin to cry, not knowing why they are so upset!

Needless to say, a night terror is a very frightening experience for parents. However, a night terror is *not* frightening for a child. That's because a night terror takes place at a very deep stage of sleep. A child does not know that it has occurred unless the parents wake him and tell him about it. Although it is hard for a parent to watch a child cry or scream this way and to feel as though there is no way to help, it is truly better for the child if parents can let the night terror run its course. The child will continue to cry, perhaps for five minutes, perhaps for as long as a half an hour. He will then go back to sleep without difficulty.

Although night terrors are common, many parents will feel shaken up by the experience. There is no reason to

121

worry about psychological causes or damage from night terrors—except for their effect on parents' peace of mind and ability to sleep peacefully themselves. If you are worried, however, a call to your health care provider in the morning may be comforting and may help you to manage the next time this difficulty occurs.

28

DAILY CARE

E very day, no matter what your plans are for yourself or your family, your two-year-old needs to become reasonably clean and get dressed. Although a few two-year-olds are cooperative and pleasant when their parents are helping them to change their clothes, wash their face and hands, take a bath, shampoo their hair, and brush their teeth, the typical two-year-old will object to some, if not all, of these activities. In this Key, you will find some ideas for helping your child to cooperate with these necessary tasks of daily living.

Always try to remember that most young children have difficulty ending one activity and beginning another. They aren't on an adult schedule, and they don't worry about making you late or being late themselves. A two-year-old is most likely to cooperate with these daily living tasks if you can make them reasonably pleasant so that she wants to participate, but structured enough so that she understands that she must follow a routine.

Getting Dressed
Getting a two-year-old dressed begins with organizing her clothing and the setting. First of all, make sure that the clothes that you expect your child to wear are comfortable, easy to put on and remove, and appealing to her. Although some children will wear anything, other children have a definite taste. If you want your child to wear a cute dress and she prefers her soft sloppy T-shirt, ask yourself, "Is this argument worth my time and energy?" Generally, a

fussy two-year-old who is given the freedom to choose her clothing for everyday play will cooperate when a parent requires special clothing for special occasions (especially if the child gets to help choose the dress-up outfit).

To simplify getting dressed in the morning, set out your child's clothes the evening before, with her help if she prefers. Remove toys and other distractions from the immediate area. Ideally, a two-year-old should be learning to dress herself with her parents' help. Realistically, most parents, especially if they have to get to work, prefer to dress their child themselves. A good compromise can be to allow your child to do one part of dressing herself on weekday mornings and more on weekends when you aren't in a rush. Many children cooperate better if they get dressed in front of a full length mirror. They can stay focussed and feel as though they are involved in dressing themselves, even if the parent is doing most of the work. Telling stories, singing songs, or using rhythmic chants, "This is the way we button our shirt, button our shirt . . ." often help to move a reluctant two-year-old towards getting dressed.

Some two-year-olds battle furiously with their parents over dressing every morning. If coaxing, games, and rituals don't work with your child, you may have to resort to holding your child down and quickly pulling her clothes on and off. If the battle occurs only on days when you are taking her to nursery school or child care, consider taking her there in her pajamas. It may be easier for the caregivers to get her cooperation. If you're lucky, she may also decide that she doesn't want to look different than the other children and be more cooperative at home the next day!

If all else fails, you can use the approach that is popular with many parents, although they are often embarrassed to tell anyone: Have your two-year-old change into her clean clothes at bedtime! You'll save time in the morning and the money you've been spending on pajamas. Your two-year-old may look a little rumpled, but rumpled clothing is a small problem compared to starting every morning with a struggle.

Baths

Most two-year-olds enjoy bathtime, even though they will sometimes object to getting into the bath at the moment you choose. Many two-year-olds will stall by fussing about details—too hot, too cold, too much water, too little, too many bubbles, not the right soap, and on and on. It's reasonable for a young child to have these preferences, but if you start to feel as though you have become lady-in-waiting to royalty, it may be that you have allowed your child to boss you around under the pretense of "getting it just right." If you have gotten into this pattern, have your child stay with you while you prepare the bath and have her participate in every detail she seems to care about. If she truly cares, she'll get involved, but if she was just fussing for attention, she'll stop her complaints.

Some two-year-olds do have very real fears about water and baths. They may be upset should you add water while they are in the tub or should you drain water before they have gotten out. These are fears that should be respected, even though they may seem silly to you. If you force a child who is truly afraid into water, she will become more resistant. Often, you can help a child to overcome her fears by having her bathe a doll and "show how to do it so the doll doesn't get scared."

A two-year-old only needs a bath when she is really dirty. If you wash her hands before eating and after using the toilet, her face once a day, and her bottom "as needed," she can get by on a weekly bath. In fact, if a child has dry or sensitive skin, it's often advisable to limit baths. If your child enjoys bubble baths, be aware that the perfume and detergent occasionally are irritating to some children's skin and may cause urinary tract infections in little girls.

Washing Hair

Two-year-olds often hate to have their hair washed, either because they don't like the feeling of leaning backwards into deep water or because they have gotten soap or water in their eyes before and remember the sting. You can prevent problems by having your child cover her face with a towel while you wash and rinse and by using "no-sting" shampoo. Singing songs and making a game out of your routine may help to distract her. Some children prefer to have their hair washed while they lie on their backs in an empty tub or on a counter with their head over the sink while a parent pours water over their hair. There's no perfect technique, but fortunately hair washing can be limited to once a week.

Brushing Teeth

A two-year-old should have her teeth brushed every night (as recommended by the American Dental Association) as part of her bedtime routine. She will probably want to brush them herself, and will enjoy the task more if you give her a decorated toothbrush with soft bristles and a cup of her own. However, you will have to finish the job for her, because she is too young to be able to brush all areas of her mouth. The best way to protect her teeth will be by using a small amount of fluoridated toothpaste and then having her swirl water around in her mouth and spitting. To increase her resistance to cavities, have her drink a glass of water a day if your local water supply has fluoride, or ask your health care provider for advice on fluoride supplements.

126

Most of these daily routines will go smoothly with your child most of the time. However, all two-year-olds will have days when they are in an uncooperative mood. You may have to choose between trying to wash your child's face and keeping your sanity! On these days, don't worry if she looks messy—mess won't hurt, and your relationship with your child in other areas is much more important than her neat appearance.

29

TOILET TRAINING DIFFICULTIES

I t would make parents' lives much easier if children grew up without much variation in how they mastered each stage of development. Of course, being parents wouldn't be very interesting if children were all the same! Nevertheless, when a child's way of being different involves being a "late bloomer" in some area of his life, or when he engages his parents in battle over an area that is trouble-free for most children, parents do get frustrated. In no area is this more true than in toilet training. Although many parents respect their child's need to be developmentally ready before starting toilet training, some children do not cooperate.

There are many different causes and reasons for children to resist toileting. In fact, the training method that works perfectly for one child in a family can be the cause of major resistance in a sibling. When a child who is clearly developmentally ready is resisting training, and parents are continually changing diapers on a child aware of his need to "go," that child's parents find themselves becoming upset. They may criticize themselves for being too easy-going or too strict in their earlier toilet training efforts, or they may find that other people are giving them advice that is confusing and contradictory. Feeling guilty won't help solve the problem, and can even make a problem worse if your guilt makes you more worried about his resistance!

One of the common problems that gets in the way of completing toilet training occurs when a child has learned to use the potty or toilet for urinating but resists having a bowel movement anywhere but in his diapers. There are a number of variations of this problem. One two-year-old will happily wear underpants until he feels the sensation of needing to have a bowel movement. He will then demand a diaper, or even go to get one himself. Another child may wait until his diaper is in place for a nap or bedtime before having a bowel movement. Another two-year-old will want to wear diapers all the time and will let parents know when he needs to pee in the potty, but go off into another part of the house to have a bowel movement in his diaper. If parents try to take the child out of diapers altogether, the child has his bowel movement in his pants, making a mess that most parents find very unpleasant.

What all of these variations have in common is that the two-year-old, who is clearly feeling the sensation of needing to have a bowel movement, and who has enough control to wait for the time and place of his choosing before he will let go, for some reason is unwilling to use the "parent-approved" site for having his bowel movement. Since successful toilet training is accomplished primarily by encouraging a child to feel competent and proud about his own ability to control his body, parents who try to force a child out of this pattern may meet with even more resistance.

There is no single solution to overcoming this type of resistance once it occurs. Most parents experiment with offering rewards and prizes for a child's cooperation, and for many children, this method is successful. However, if you find yourself trying different methods to get your child to cooperate and your child continues to resist, it's a good idea to ease up on the pressure. Children can have many reasons for resisting the final steps of toilet training, and a child whose parent focuses too much on this task may wind up developing even stronger and more long-lasting resistance. For this reason, if you feel that you and your child have "tried everything" and you are not making any progress, it makes sense to tell your child that he can continue his pattern for now, and you'll wait until he is older to take any further steps. Stop urging your child in any way to change his toileting habits for at least six weeks. At that point, try again. If you are still getting nowhere, or if your child is acting upset, angry, or defiant about the issue, talk to your health care provider. It is often helpful to get an outside person's view of the situation, and many two-year-olds respond very well to the interest and attention of the person their parents consult for help.

A less common type of resistance to toilet training, but one that is more serious, is when a child refuses to have any bowel movement at all. A two-year-old can have enough control to withhold his bowel movement for several days at a time. This withholding is a problem because when a child waits too long to have a bowel movement, he is likely to become constipated. The stools he withholds will become hard, dry, and more difficult to pass the longer he waits to try. If you see this pattern emerging, it's important to take three actions. The first is to ease up on any pressure you have placed on your child to be toilet trained or to use the potty in a certain way. The second is to increase the amount of high fiber foods you offer your child, so that his bowel movements will stay soft: fruit, whole grains, and cereals with added bran are popular high-fiber foods for two-year-olds. Third, observe your child for any evidence that having a bowel movement is painful or uncomfortable for him. If you see him grunting or looking as though he has a stomach-ache before he has a bowel movement, make an appointment with your health care provider to discuss this pattern. By taking this last action, you can avoid having your child develop a more serious problem of resistance to toilet training, that of stool retention and soiling.

When a young child continues to withhold his bowel movements and becomes constipated, the hard bowel movement hurts when he finally passes it. In order to avoid another painful experience, the child tries to hold on as long as he can to each bowel movement. In holding on, the bowel movements become larger and harder and, of course, more painful to pass. If this pattern continues, a child's lower bowel can become stretched and the nerves that signal "time to go" become less sensitive. This condition will usually become worse if left untreated and can even result in a child having involuntary leaking and soiling of liquid bowel movement that seep out around the hard mass of constipated stools. In addition, the constipation can cause a child to have accidents with urination as well. If you suspect that your child may be developing this condition, it is essential that you make an appointment with your child's health care provider. Before your appointment, keep a record of your child's toileting pattern, noting the time, size, and consistency of each bowel movement. In most cases, a child with this problem will need to take medicine to soften and lubricate his bowel movements for an extended period of time. As troublesome as this problem can be, it is one that can be resolved with good medical supervision.

Occasionally, a two-year-old will simply refuse to try to use the toilet for bowel movements or urination, even though parents have observed that he is able to hold on for several hours at a time. Sometimes the child may have stayed dry or used the potty for several days in response to rewards, but then returned to using diapers after the novelty of new toys or stickers wore off. The child may tell his parents that he'll use the potty "when I'm bigger" but not now. Although this resistance is very frustrating for parents, it's better to avoid arguing with your child about when he's going to be "big enough." However, it is often helpful to look at other aspects of your child's daily life to make sure that you are not sending him mixed messages about whether you really think he is "big." A two-year-old who is still being changed on a changing table, using a bottle, being carried, or sleeping in a crib may still be thinking of himself as a baby. A child who is being treated like a "big boy" is often more willing to take "big boy" steps on his own.

Most children don't struggle with their parents about toilet training, but some do. Because so much of your life with a two-year-old is spent on caretaking tasks like diapering, a prolonged struggle with toilet training can make you feel tired and even inadequate as a parent. It's important to remember that all two-year-olds struggle with parents about one thing or another, and whatever energy you are putting into this issue is being taken up by another issue in another family!

30

READING TO YOUR TWO-YEAR-OLD

Even though your child is only two years old, he is learning words, concepts, and ideas at a faster rate now than he will ever learn them again in his whole life. As his parent, you can take advantage of this rapid learning by giving your child a head start on the most important skill he will need to be successful in school: reading.

Parents who read to their children regularly set the foundation for their child's learning to read later on. How do they do this? Picture you and your child reading together. Your child is sitting next to you, or in your lap. You open a picture book and start to read together—yes, *together*. Of course, your two-year-old won't be able to figure out what each word means—he may be six or seven years old before he can do that. But he will be learning a lot more about reading than many parents realize.

First of all, he will be learning about position and direction. He will learn how to hold a book right-side up, and how to read a book so that the pictures and stories make sense from beginning to end. In this way, he gradually learns about left-to-right movement.

He will be learning that the black markings on the pages are symbols for words. He will start to recognize that within the clusters of black marks there are marks that repeat, and that he sees those marks in other places. If he has seen his own name written many times, he may even begin to recognize that the marks match letters that stand for himself. For a two-year-old who is still learning about the magic of speech, realizing that marks can "talk" is very exciting!

As you read to your child, he will hear the words he knows used in many different ways. He will also learn new words, some of which might be different than the ones he hears in everyday life. A child who is read to builds a much larger vocabulary because he is exposed to more words. Since the words are part of a story, he can learn to figure out the meaning of the words in context, either on his own or by asking you "What's that?" When a child learns a new word in this way he is much more likely to remember it than if he has to memorize it for a spelling or vocabulary test in school. Some two-year-olds love the big picture books that label all of the items. If your child is attracted to these books, by all means read them to him. He may begin to point to and label the pictures himself. Although this label recognition is not the same as true reading, the interest that your child is showing will help him want to read in the years to come.

A child who is read to can also learn the ways that speech can differ among people from different backgrounds. You can find books about people from many other countries and ethnic groups, stories that are written in English but whose word patterns and rhythm reflect the diversity of the world. A two-year-old can travel to New York, to New Mexico, to Africa, China, and England without leaving your lap!

Your child will also learn the rhythm of language, and the special beats of rhyming poems or repetitive stories.

Most two-year-olds will love books that have lines that reappear throughout the book, and your child will love to say the line with you, or even all by himself. As you read, say each word carefully and pace yourself slowly so that your child can hear each word and phrase distinctly.

The most important reason for parents to read to a young child, however, is that by linking your attention and closeness to the act of reading, your child will learn at this early age that reading is fun. He will attach his feelings of loving you to the special time of listening to you read. For your child to be a successful reader, he has to want to read. If reading reminds him of a loving time with his parent, he will be able to recapture that feeling when he opens a book on his own.

A two-year-old doesn't need a large number of books, but the ones he has should be carefully selected. Most two-year-olds will prefer books about familiar, everyday subjects, especially children and families. They often love books that substitute animals for people. Some children like books about topics that are special to them, such as trains or trucks. The illustrations should be clear and simple, and colored pictures are often appealing. However, if you are going to buy a beautifully illustrated children's book, be sure to read the story to yourself first. Make sure that the story and vocabulary are at your child's level, or he may not be interested. One or two sentences on each page is about right for a two-year-old, and the story should be simple and easy to follow. You can also "tell" a story to your child while you look at the pictures, and add the actual reading as your child gets older.

Keep the books you own in a safe place, and have some simple rules about caring for them. Most two-year-olds will need to be taught that the paper in a book is not for tearing or scribbling. If your child does damage a book, put his books in a safer place for a while, but don't punish your child by refusing to read to him or by not letting him have any books at all. Give him his books one at a time and supervise him until you are sure that he can remember the rules on his own.

Your local library is a wonderful and free source of books for your two-year-old. Most libraries will have a special section of books for the very young. Some libraries even have toddler story times, for children too young to listen for more than a few minutes. A two-year-old's attention span is short, and parents shouldn't worry if reading time lasts for less time than it takes to find a book and get settled on the rug. If you make regular visits to the library, your child will learn to feel comfortable in the "house of books," as one two-year-old described his local library.

If it seems like a lot of extra work to organize reading time for your child, remember that the benefits for a child who loves books will last his lifetime! If you are lucky, the benefits will come soon. Many parents have been amazed to find their two- or three-year-old child sitting quietly in his room with a pile of books, "reading" the familiar stories that he has memorized from the many times his parents read them to him!

31

THE TWO-YEAR-OLD AND THE NEW BABY

When a new baby arrives in a two-year-old's family it is quite natural for parents to feel, at times, as though they can't give enough energy or attention to either child. In fact, many parents begin to worry during pregnancy, "Will we be able to love and care for two children?" Even though it is exciting to be having a baby, their two-year-old is at such an exciting stage of life that parents may wonder if their second child will be as interesting as their first. Even after the baby is born, the contrast between the two children, each at different stages of development and with different needs, can cause parents to feel torn. "Do I go to the baby who is crying or the toddler who is screaming?" "Do I make the baby wait to nurse or make my two-year-old wait for lunch?" "Should I wake the baby to take his big brother to the park, or should we stay home even though we've been indoors all day?"

These worries can make family life stressful for everyone, especially the two-year-old who is adjusting to having to share his parents' attention with the new arrival. It's often helpful to realize that most parents of two or more children share your feelings and have the same difficulties as you do. Usually, as parents relax and lower their expectations of how much they can do for each child, family life becomes easier to manage.

When you have a two-year-old, the most important step you can take towards preparing and caring for your second child is to plan for extra help for Mom during the first month or two after the new baby arrives. Because babies are unpredictable in their needs during this period and two-year-olds do best on a fairly routine schedule, it's very hard for one parent to take care of two without exhausting herself. Unless Dad has a flexible schedule and can take some time off from work, Mom needs some help at home, even if it's just for an hour or two a day. The helper can be a family member, a friend, or a "mother's helper" such as a teenager who comes in after school. Ideally, the helper should help with housework or be able to care for the children so that Mom can take a rest. This kind of help may sound like a luxury, but mothers who get enough help in the early post-partum weeks regain their health and energy much faster than mothers who try to do everything alone. When a family takes good care of Mom it's like putting money into an emotional bank account!

Some two-year-olds are very accepting of a new baby's arrival. However, most will show some feelings of distress, either in the first few weeks following the baby's birth or in the months that follow. Sometimes it takes a two-year-old a while to realize that this new family member is a permanent addition. Often, the two-year-old doesn't seem to be bothered until the younger one is old enough to crawl around or grab at the older child's toys.

When a two-year-old feels threatened by a new baby, he may express feelings of anger towards his parents. It's as if he were saying, "I trusted you to be all mine! Now, look what you've done to me!" However, since he is too young to be able to tell his parents how he feels, and is probably unable to understand why he feels angry or left out, he may act out his feelings in a number of different ways.

The most common reaction to a new baby that you will see in a two-year-old is *regression*. Regression means that your child "goes backwards" in his development, most often by seeming to lose the skills that he has most recently acquired. The typical forms of regression you might see in your child at this age include talking "baby-talk," wanting to be fed, losing toileting skills, or demanding to be held like a baby. Although this regression can be very annoying to parents who already have their arms filled with one baby, your older child really needs you to accept his behavior. For example, if your child begins to have toileting accidents, you can say, "Oh, I guess you forgot that you're not wearing diapers anymore." If your child is resistant to toileting, you may choose to put him back into diapers for a few weeks. Be sure that this is not done in a punitive way. Rather, say something like, "Let's not worry about this for now. When the baby is older and you're older, we'll try again." If your child is talking or acting babyish, you can say, "It's fun to pretend to be a baby, isn't it?" You can also point out to your child how much you enjoy the things he can do, because he is older: "It's fun to hold you and rock you, but I like it that you're old enough to sing silly songs with me, too!"

Another common reaction to a new baby is directing angry or provocative behavior towards parents. Although the behavior may not seem to have anything to do with the new baby, especially since two-year-olds are often provocative anyway, parents should talk to their child about how he is feeling. An older child is sometimes testing his parents: "Do you still love me, even though you've brought that baby into our home?" "Are the rules going to change for me, now that I have to share my room and your attention?" Parents need to set firm limits on their two-year-old's behavior, but at the same time reassure him that they still love him and that he doesn't have to worry about being replaced. A parent might respond to an angry outburst, "I know that it's hard when you have to wait for me when I'm feeding the baby. You can get mad, but I won't let you hit me or throw a toy." A parent can also say, "It's a lot of work to take care of a baby. I get tired and so do you. Sometimes I wish it weren't so hard. But even if I get angry or you get angry, I still love you."

Parents can help a two-year-old to understand the new baby's needs by talking to their older child about how they took care of him when he was a baby. Your older child can look at pictures of himself being held and fed when he was little. You can tell your child, "This is how we took care of you when you were a baby. We want to take care of this baby just like we cared for you, so that he will grow up to be as nice and healthy as you are."

Although life with a two-year-old and a new baby will be very hectic, if you take good care of yourselves you may find that the two year spacing is very convenient. Your children may be very different in personalities and interests, but children who are less than three years apart are usually able to play together well as they get older. The early years of nonstop work are eventually forgotten when your children are finally old enough to play basketball or a board game together while you relax in another room!

32

~~~~~~

ANGER AND AGGRESSION

"When Sarah gets angry she hits anyone who's near. I get furious, and then I feel bad that I'm as out of control as she is." "When Jason gets that 'look' I feel like a failure. How can he get so mad when I've tried to make everything just right for him?"

Everyone gets angry, whether they are young or old. When people feel angry, tension builds up inside them around that anger, and it needs to be released. If anger is either held in or released in a destructive way, the angry person will continue to feel bad or will do things that make other people angry. However, children or adults can learn to release their anger by expressing it in a way that doesn't hurt themselves or other people. They can learn that they can get angry, feel bad, and then be free to experience other, more pleasant feelings.

A two-year-old can't understand or think through his feelings very well. He learns to express himself by watching his parents and the way they react to him and to other people. If you want to help your child express anger in a healthy, acceptable way, you'll have to begin by reflecting for a moment on your own childhood. Think about your parents and how they dealt with anger. Did they ever let you see them get angry? Did they express a lot of anger? Did they get angry at you, perhaps unfairly? How did they react when you were angry? Did they allow you to feel angry or did they get angry back? Did they try to talk to you or did they ignore your feelings? If you were taught as a child that expressing anger is "bad," you may need to learn some ways to help yourself and your child express anger without causing harm.

In order to express your anger in a healthy, nonhurtful way, you and your child must first learn to recognize the feelings that mean, "I'm angry" before they burst out. Then, you must learn ways of acting angry that don't trigger angry reactions from other people. Finally, you must learn to come up with solutions to the problem that caused the anger.

A two-year-old needs to learn words to label his emotions. A parent can help him learn by using words to describe feelings. In addition to telling your child when you are happy, sad, or angry, you can label his own expressions of emotion with words: "I can see by your big smile that you're happy now!" "You look so angry when your face is all turned down like that." You can talk about characters in the stories you read, labelling their feelings with words. You can use stuffed animals or puppets to tell your child stories, making up situations that show how the characters express their feelings through their actions.

As you use these ways to teach your child the words for feelings, you can also talk about the ways that the feelings can best be expressed. You could tell your child that when you get mad you feel better if you stamp your feet, "but what would happen if, when I stamped my feet, I stamped so hard that I broke my toe? or broke the floor? or stamped on the cat?" In this way, you show your child that expressing anger is okay, but that you are careful not to hurt people or things when you express yourself. You could make up a puppet story where a puppet gets angry and

142

hurts someone and then the other puppets become angry, too. You could then have the first angry puppet use words to say, "I'm angry and I need help." The other puppets could then help and be sympathetic. Although these techniques may seem contrived or elaborate, in practice they only take an extra minute or two as you play or talk with your child. Parents who use these techniques report that their children enjoy the storytelling and play and often learn quickly the concepts the parents are teaching them.

As your two-year-old develops her ability to use language to communicate, you can help her to learn to solve the problems that underlie anger. Using the storytelling or puppet play methods, you can suggest ways in which characters can cope with anger by figuring out solutions. For example, a puppet could be angry because he has to go home while his friends are still playing. A puppet mother could be understanding of the anger and ask, "What can we do to solve this problem?" The angry child puppet could make suggestions and the mother and child might agree to arrange another play date. Another good way for young children to express themselves is by using physical activity to release energy: hitting pillows or a punching bag, running around, yelling loud (not at someone else), or crying hard. A parent can tell a two-year-old, "When you're angry, you can tell me in words, but if words aren't enough, here are things you can do." After the child gets the feelings out, the parent can say, "Now, let's talk about solving this problem." Children can also use art materials to express themselves: pounding clay or painting or coloring on big pieces of paper can be an outlet for strong emotions. A child may even use art to tell a story that includes a solution to the problem that triggered the anger. By letting your child know that these ways of showing anger are understandable and acceptable to you, you show your child that he can express himself without being scolded or shamed.

It is helpful for children to have family guidelines for expressing anger, guidelines that all members of the family can accept and follow. An easy rule for young children to understand is, "In our family, we don't hurt people or things." As a child gets older, you can teach him that words sometimes hurt, and that even when he is angry you don't want him to use words that are hurtful. Gradually, a child can learn to say, "I hate it when she knocks down my blocks!" instead of "I hate her!" To be effective, parents must not just teach these guidelines, but model them themselves.

When your child hits or hurts someone physically, you can remind him of the rule. If his behavior is unusual, you may want immediately to try to find out what has caused him to act that way. But if your child often has trouble controlling his impulse to hit, kick, or bite, you may want to give him a brief time-out for the behavior and then deal with his feelings. You can ask him to use words to tell you, or the person with whom he is angry, how he feels. Then, you can give him time to calm down and give yourself time to figure out what to do next. You may be able to help him solve the problem that caused his anger. You may have to let him know that you accept and understand his anger but that you can't fix the problem. Either way, your child will be comforted by knowing that you understand.

Sometimes parents feel that their two-year-olds are acting angry and using aggressive behavior for no apparent reason. They see their child lashing out at others with words or fists without being provoked. Their child doesn't seem to be able to say why he is angry, and perhaps doesn't even seem angry after his outbursts. Sometimes, this kind of anger is a result of the child being under stress from a life event that is making him worried or unhappy—such as a parent's illness, a change in childcare, or the birth of a sibling. Talking to other parents, a teacher, or your health care provider may help you to figure out if there is a broader issue to consider. However, if you can't identify an obvious source of stress in your child's life, it is worthwhile to look at your overall pattern of dealing with your child's behavior for a clue. Some children who "act angry" are actually using aggressive behavior as a way of getting their parents to impose limits. It's as if they are saying, "I know you won't say 'no' to me when I'm bossy, demanding, or rude, but I know you'll stop me if I slap you in the face. Won't you please take charge?" If you see yourself as a kind, loving parent whose child who is often acting angry, this may be the cause of the behavior he is expressing. Read the Keys on Discipline and Responding to Misbehavior. By working on your overall approach to your child's behavior, you may be able to eliminate this particular misbehavior.

33

CHOOSING CHILDCARE

When you decide that your two-year-old is ready to spend time on a regular basis with other children, you will need to find a play group, preschool, or childcare program that is suitable for him. Young children usually take a while to adjust to a group setting, and they don't like to make a lot of changes. It's a good idea to spend time visiting the programs that are available in your area so that you can find a place that you think will suit your child for now and perhaps for the next two to three years. It's not easy to find quality childcare programs. There are no nationwide standards for most childcare except for minimal health and safety regulations. If you want your child to be happy and well cared for, you will have to observe the setting carefully so that you can be sure that the caregivers, the environment, and the program plan are up to your own standards for your child.

Begin your search for a quality program by asking friends for recommendations. You can also ask your health care provider for suggestions. Many communities have a childcare information and referral service that lists programs that meet local licensing standards. You probably will find that you hear about the same programs from different people, which may be reassuring. However, there is no substitute for visiting on your own, since people differ in their values about what makes a program good. Call the programs and set up appointments to visit. A quality program will welcome your observation and will not try to restrict your visiting time to times when children are not present or are asleep. To evaluate a program, you must be there at times when the children and caregivers are interacting. You will probably need to stay for forty-five minutes to an hour to get enough information to guide your decision.

When you make your visits, you will find it helpful to take paper and pencil and a list of questions that will help you to evaluate the program. Here are some questions that can serve as a guide:

- What are your first impressions about the program? Do they change after a short visit? Parents should trust their feelings about a program, even if they aren't sure why they like or don't like what they see.
- Do the children seem to be playing happily? Are they engaging in activities and with each other? Although every child will have moments of unhappiness in a normal day, you shouldn't see children who look sad or withdrawn for more than a short time.
- Do the caregivers seem to be enjoying the children and are they interacting comfortably with them? Are they showing affection and warmth in their words and actions? The caregivers are the key to your child's feelings about himself, and their attitude is more important than the activities or equipment that the program provides.
- Is the space large enough to allow children to play actively? Is there an outdoor area with riding toys, climbing equipment, a sand area, and room to run and jump? Is the area clean and well-maintained? Is the outdoor play well-supervised? Young children need space, not just for play but to provide them with room to discharge energy. When children are crowded together, they are more likely to push and shove and behave aggressively.

- Are there different activity areas for the children? A quality program will provide opportunities for children to engage in many different activities throughout the day. Typical areas will include:
  - *Block corner:* Wooden blocks, cardboard blocks, milk-carton blocks, and blocks made out of boxes provide children with imaginative ways to construct buildings. You may see other toys in this area that the children can use in their play: toy cars or trains, farm animals, pretend people, or dinosaurs. Observe how the children play here. Are they generally cooperative and industrious or do they seem to have trouble sharing and playing together?
  - *Kitchen/dress-up area:* Young children like to pretend to be grown-ups, and they need to have a place with equipment and clothing that triggers dramatic play. Baby dolls and toys are often found in this area so that children can play "family." Watch how children share and interact here, and notice what happens when a new child wants to join in.
  - *Puzzles/manipulative toys:* You should see an area where children can play with small toys that encourage them to use their rapidly increasing fine motor skills. Simple puzzles, large beads and string, toys that interlock, and peg boards are examples of the items you should see in this area. There should be space on the floor or at a low table for children to work, and the toys should be neatly arranged in baskets or on shelves so that the children can take them out and help to put them away when they are finished.
  - *Story/quiet corner:* Look for a comfortable space where children can look at picture books or have some quiet time. At times throughout the day, a caregiver should be spending time in this area

reading to children. Even if the program has a regular group story time, a quality program will provide an opportunity for children to have extra book and story time in a cozier setting.

- *Arts/crafts project areas:* Young children are messy when they create art, so you should see an area where they are allowed to paint and use art materials without having to be too careful. Some programs will set up special projects for an hour, others will have easels, paper, crayons, or paint available throughout the day. The best art projects for young children are those that encourage the child to express himself without worrying about the final product. Two-year-olds are too young to make pictures of real objects, although they may tell you a long story about a picture they made that looks like scribbles or splotches to someone else.

• What are the special times in the program?

- *Arrival time:* When the children arrive, are they greeted by a caregiver, signed in, and given time to say good-bye to their parents? In a quality program you will see caregivers giving attention to children who are having trouble separating from parents.

- *Transition times:* Most young children have some difficulty ending one activity and beginning another. Do you see providers assisting children by giving them signals such as ringing a bell, giving quiet reminders, or providing a ritual, such as a song or a game, to move the group along? Children who are having difficulty with transitions should be helped, not scolded, if they resist.

- *Story/circle time:* Most two-year-olds will enjoy a brief time for group stories or songs. Some two-year-olds will need to stand up or move about while listening. Does the circle time look like fun and are fidgety children welcomed in the group?

- *Snack/meal time:* Are you comfortable with the type of food and the manner of serving? Most two-year-olds are particular about what they eat and how food is presented to them. If the time for eating is orderly and calm and the food that is served is appetizing, children who are hungry will be better able to relax and eat.

• What are health and hygiene policies? Two-year-olds who enter group settings are likely to have an increased number of colds and other minor illnesses, especially during the winter months. A quality program protects children by having staff and children wash hands after diapering and toileting and before handling food. Bathroom and diapering areas are kept clean and toys are washed and disinfected as needed. Children's runny noses are wiped and paper or fresh cloth towels are available for children to wash and dry their hands and faces. Each child's bedding is kept clean and separate.

• Has the program done a thorough job of child-proofing indoors and out? Are unsafe materials locked out of reach? Are electrical cords and cleaning and cooking equipment put away safely? Is there enough supervisory staff to handle an emergency? In most states, an evacuation plan for fire or other disasters is required of all licensed caregivers, and you should ask to see it.

After you choose a program, it's a good idea to continue to visit your child while he is in care. *All* programs should welcome parents to visit at any time, with no restrictions. Any program that limits parental access is not a safe place for your child. A quality program will want you to drop by anytime, because the best childcare providers want parents to see and appreciate what a good job they are doing, all day and every day.

34

WEANING FROM THE
BOTTLE

Some two-year-olds are attached to drinking from a bottle. They enjoy sucking, and they also enjoy the good feelings that they associate with the bottle, feelings of being cared for like a little baby. Some parents have encouraged the use of a bottle to keep their toddler occupied during car rides or to help them comfort themselves when they were unhappy, thinking that the child would outgrow his need for it. However, if your two-year-old has not voluntarily given up his bottle by now, there are some good reasons to help him break the "bottle habit."

The most important reason for weaning a child from a bottle is to protect his teeth. When a child sucks from a bottle, the liquid collects right behind his front teeth. All liquids, except water, contain natural sugars that are metabolized by the bacteria present in the mouth. When these sugars are metabolized, an acid is produced that is very damaging to the enamel coating of brand new teeth. Once this enamel is damaged, your child is likely to get cavities that can be painful and require extensive repair.

A second problem associated with drinking from a bottle is poor eating habits. Some two-year-olds who enjoy drinking milk or juice from a bottle tend to fill up on these liquids rather than eat regular meals and snacks. Other children eat well in addition to drinking from a bottle and gain too much weight for their age and height. When parents limit or eliminate the milk and juice their child takes from a bottle, they usually find that his overall eating habits improve.

Of course, many parents are reluctant to take away a toddler's bottle because they feel that he is dependent on it for comfort. A two-year-old may use his bottle as a lovey or transitional object, as you will read about in the next Key. However, the bottle is such a powerful symbol of being a baby that it has certain disadvantages to a growing child. Parents who offer their child a bottle throughout the day may notice that their two-year-old often acts more "babyish" than other children his age. Once their child is weaned they may notice that he is acting more like a confident two-year-old, because they are treating him as one.

If you want to wean your two-year-old from the bottle, there are several methods that work well. One method is to gradually dilute the contents of your child's bottles with water, replacing one ounce of milk or juice with one ounce of water every other day (some parents dilute at the rate of one half-ounce every day). You don't need to tell your child, and some children don't seem to notice. At the end of two weeks, your child will be getting a bottle of water only, and you will not have to be concerned about problems with his teeth or his appetite. Many children whose parents use this method become less interested in the bottle at this point and stop using it on their own.

A few children, however, get very upset and angry when their parents use the dilution method. Whether or not they see the parent adding water, they taste the difference and they don't like it. Some parents can use the method anyway, saying matter-of-factly, "This is how I'm fixing your bottle today. You don't have to drink it if you don't want to." However, if you find that the dilution method is turning into a power struggle that continues day after day, your child will probably do better by having you limit bottle use, either gradually or all at once.

If you want to limit bottle use gradually, tell your child that he may only have the bottle at certain times and in certain places. Parents who use this method usually offer the bottle in the morning or evening and perhaps at naptime. They don't allow the child to walk around with the bottle or "snack" from it. They limit the number of bottles and perhaps the amount they put in each bottle. Although most two-year-olds will initially protest when you set limits on their use of the bottle, they will eventually accept the new rules. Over time, you can decrease the number of bottles until you feel your child is ready to be weaned completely.

To eliminate bottle use entirely, tell your child in a calm and confident tone that you have decided that he isn't going to have any more bottles. You can set a date for the "last bottle." Some parents tell a child a day before, some a week before. Although you don't want to take this step at a time when your family is making a major change, such as starting new childcare or moving, don't wait for a completely calm time—life will never be that calm! Gather all of the bottles and nipples in the house and throw them out, because if you don't, you will have trouble resisting your child when he protests. Most two-year-olds will be angry at first and demand that you change your mind. However, after a few days, the demands will lessen, and at the end of a week your child will be used to the new routine. As hard as the weaning may be for parents, it's usually much easier for the two-year-old!

35

LOVEYS AND TRANSITIONAL OBJECTS

I f you've ever seen the comic strip "Peanuts" you know about loveys and transitional objects. Linus, Charlie Brown's wise adviser and Lucy's victimized little brother, often carries a special blanket around with him. The blanket is his stability, allowing him the strength to deal with Charlie Brown's anxiety and Lucy's criticism. Many young children are just like Linus—independent, intelligent, and capable, but at the same time needy of a special object that helps them to feel strong. Some parents worry that their child's dependence on a blanket, a teddy bear, or some other cozy comforter is a sign of insecurity. However, many children are dependent on loveys throughout their early years, and these children are no more likely to be insecure than children who don't have a special comfort habit. Parents shouldn't worry, but they may want to make some rules about when and where the lovey can be used as their child gets older.

Most children who have a lovey need these objects in order to fall asleep at night and at naptime. They may also want them at times throughout the day, especially if they are tired or unhappy. Some two-year-olds want to take their lovey everywhere, treating the lovey like a friend or companion. One two-year-old girl had a blanket named

Texas who was as much a part of the family as a second child. Another two-year-old wasn't interested in carrying a blanket or teddy bear around with him, but he attached himself to a special sweater that he wore on cold days and wrapped around his neck when the weather was warm.

Of course, the more places you allow your child to take her lovey, the more opportunities she will have to lose it. For some children, the loss of a beloved stuffed animal or blankie is truly devastating. For this reason, some parents tell a child that she can only have her lovey when she is at home. Other parents try to find a duplicate item, and have the child use both so that the familiar softness and smell make the objects interchangeable if one is lost. When the lovey is a blanket, some parents cut off a portion to be portable while the main part stays at home.

If your child is in a childcare program, she may need to take her lovey with her, even if she is otherwise only allowed to have it at home. A child who is away from home for long periods often treasures her special object even more, because it provides a tangible link in the child's memory to her home. However, participants in a group setting will have to be even more careful than parents about protecting the child's lovey. The most appropriate rules for a group setting usually involve keeping the object in the child's cubbie except for naptime or other quiet times, and telling children that they cannot take the objects outside. Again, these limits are set to protect the objects, and not because it is inappropriate for a two-year-old to be strongly attached to them at this age.

One type of lovey that sometimes worries parents is the pacifier. An older child who has become attached to this method of comforting herself may demand that she have a pacifier available at all times. Some young children will walk around all day with a pacifier in their mouths, or refuse to go to sleep, ride in the car, or even listen to a story without this special object. At this age, pacifier use is unlikely to affect a child's teeth or jaw development, as parents sometimes fear. However, the *constant* use of a pacifier may interfere with a child's social and emotional development if she uses the pacifier to "plug" herself up at times when she could be talking or expressing feelings. Many parents find that this is a good age to limit pacifier use to certain times, such as nap or rest time, bedtime, or times when the child is winding down from a long day. At other times, the pacifier is put away and if the child needs comfort she is given extra attention and cuddling. After a child has become used to doing without a pacifier most of the time, parents can decide whether they want to eliminate its use altogether. If you decide that your child should not have a pacifier at all, be sure to choose a time that is free from other stresses or changes in her life to announce your decision. On a day that you choose, tell your child that it is time to say good-bye to the pacifier and then get rid of all the pacifiers in the house. Once this is accomplished, you can expect your child to be very unhappy and to need a great deal of extra attention as she makes the transition to life without a pacifier.

Whatever the item is that your child loves, your rules for its use should be based on your child's need for it and the practical aspects of allowing or restricting its use. Although no one can predict at what age your child will voluntarily give up her lovey, there is no evidence that these objects are in any way damaging to her growth and development.

QUESTIONS AND ANSWERS

Our two-year-old enjoys playing at home and going on short excursions with us or his baby-sitter. Does he need to be in a nursery school, or is this sufficient?

Many two-year-olds are quite happy to spend most of their time with adults, especially if they can play occasionally with other children at a park or on visits. Sometime this year, your child will probably start to enjoy getting together with other children more often. A two-year-old does not need to go to nursery school for educational reasons, but organized programs are an easy way for children to get together and play. You may want to involve your child in an informal play group or start exchanging visits with some children and families whose company you enjoy.

Our daughter is a very picky eater. How can I get her to eat vegetables?

Try not to struggle with your daughter about her food choices. Putting pressure on her will only cause her to resist you more. When you prepare her meals include tastes of vegetables and fruits, but at the same time offer her wholesome foods that she enjoys. If a two-year-old has a bowl of cereal and milk for dinner instead of chicken and corn, she'll survive quite nicely! Do limit sweet and fatty

157

foods, because they will fill her up and she won't be hungry for more nutritious foods. If your daughter refuses to eat any fruits or vegetables at all for over a month, you can start to give her a children's multi-vitamin tablet for your own peace of mind.

Some people say that when a child is on a "time-out" you should make them stop crying before the time-out ends. My child often cries for ten minutes.

Parents who try to make a child stop crying before he can end a time-out often wind up in prolonged battles. The purpose of a "time-out" is to interrupt the child's misbehavior, not to punish him for being upset. I have heard of parents keeping two-year-olds in "time-out" for hours. This seems pointless, since most young children quickly forget the reason they were put in a "time-out" in the first place.

Our two-year-old son is big for his age and fairly active as well. He is easy to get along with at home, but when he is with other children he often pushes and shoves them. He seems surprised when they cry.

Many two-year-olds push or shove other children because they are feeling crowded or because the other children are in their way. A two-year-old's natural self-centered way of thinking makes it hard for him to understand that when he pushes, another child might be hurt. Until your child is old enough to control himself better, it would be best to stay very close to him in situations where he is playing with other children. Try to catch him before he pushes or shoves, and remind him to play gently. If he does hurt another child, don't scold him harshly. Instead, remove him from the group for a moment to remind him to be gentle, and then stay next to him to help him control himself.

Our two-year-old usually speaks in two or three word sentences. He has lots of single words, and seems to understand everything we say to him. But our friends have children the same age who are chattering all the time, in long, complicated sentences! Should we be worried?

Two-year-olds vary widely in their rate of language development. The words, sentences, and understanding you are describing in your two-year-old are just fine for his age. He should continue to develop at his own pace, and it's likely that in another year his language skills will be equal to your friend's children. Continue to talk to him, to read to him, and to listen to him, but don't worry.

If I'm feeling tired or have a headache, my two-year-old daughter seems to get very worried. She tries to pat my head and says, "Mamma OK?" I don't want to make her upset, but it's hard to hide the way I feel.

It sounds as if your daughter is very sensitive to your moods and the expressions on your face. She may be the kind of child who is sensitive in general and notices things that other children ignore. A two-year-old can worry when her mother doesn't seem to be herself because she wonders, "If my Mommy isn't OK, who will take care of me?" You can best reassure her by telling her that even if you're tired or sick, you can take good care of her. If you find that you need to nap or rest during the day, be sure to have someone supervise your daughter if you can't, since a two-year-old can get into trouble very quickly when a parent is distracted.

Should we let our two-year-old watch cartoons on TV?

TV cartoon adventure shows often show characters who fight and use violence as a way of solving most problems. Although it's hard to predict if a two-year-old will be harmed by these shows, it is worthwhile for parents to ask themselves whether they think that the shows will help their children in any way. A two-year-old is young enough to be unsure of whether what he watches on television is real or not. It is common for young children to believe that the characters they see in that special box in the living room are as real as the characters they see in their own homes or in their neighborhoods. Although a two-year-old may play pretend games, he doesn't always know that he is pretending. Therefore, you should assume that whatever he sees happening on the television screen will influence him just as the events in his daily life do.

If my child thinks that the characters on TV are real, does that mean he shouldn't watch television at all?

Not at all. Some television shows, especially the ones shown on public television stations, are designed to entertain very young children without showing characters behaving violently and aggressively. These shows often show children or pretend characters facing a problem and working out a positive solution with help from friends and grown-ups. In addition, these shows also tell stories and teach pre-reading and counting skills in ways that most young children enjoy. Pre-school teachers report that children who regularly watch these shows seem to be more advanced in these areas than children who do not.

It seems that whenever I ask my two-year-old to do something she says "no." I'm tired of hearing that word!

The word "no" is such a part of a normal two-year-old's vocabulary that it's unlikely you'll be able to get her to stop saying it at all. However, you can try to avoid asking her questions that give her the chance to say no as easily.

For example, instead of beginning a sentence with "Do you want to . . ." try, "Let's do . . ." or "Now it's time to . . . ." Instead of asking your daughter if she wants something, present her with a choice: "Do you want your red shirt or your blue shirt?" She won't give up saying "no," but you may hear that word less.

How can I get my two-year-old to pick up his toys?

Most two-year-olds will not pick up toys on their own. If you want your child to participate in cleaning up, it's best to have clean-up time be a regular part of each day. Have a routine or a game, such as your picking up a toy and handing it to him to place on a shelf, or taking turns putting toys away, one at a time. Also, if your child has too many toys to play with, he'll make a bigger mess. It's easier for both of you if you limit the number of toys he can play with. If you rotate his toys, putting away some and bringing out others, he'll think they're new and you won't have as big of a clean-up job.

SUGGESTED READING
AND RESOURCES

Brazelton, T. Berry. *Toddlers and Parents*. New York: Dell Publishing Co., 1989.

Ferber, Richard. *Solve Your Child's Sleep Problems*. New York: Simon and Schuster, Inc., 1985.

Kurcinka, Mary Sheedy. *Raising Your Spirited Child*. New York: HarperCollins, 1991.

Satter, Ellyn. *How to Get Your Kid to Eat . . . But Not Too Much*. Palo Alto, California: Bull Publishing Co., 1987.

Van der Zande, Irene. *1, 2, 3 . . The Toddler Years*. Santa Cruz Toddler Care Center, 1738 16th Avenue, Santa Cruz, California 95062, 1986.

Zweiback, Meg. *Keys to Preparing and Caring for Your Second Child*. New York: Barron's Educational Series, 1991.

Child Help: National Child Abuse Hotline (24-hour resource and referral for parents under stress): 1-800-422-4453.

GLOSSARY

Auditory learner   a child or person who learns best by listening.

Constipation   hard or dry bowel movements. Irregular, soft bowel movements are common in two-year-olds and are not signs of constipation.

Nightmare   a dream that causes a child to wake up tearful or afraid and usually in need of comfort.

Night terror   a partial arousal from sleep that causes the child to thrash about, scream, or cry. The child is calm as soon as he is fully awake and does not seem afraid.

Temperament   the inborn behavioral style that influences the way a child interacts with his caregivers and the environment.

Tactile learner   a child or person who learns best by touching.

Visual learner   a child or person who learns best by observing or watching.

INDEX